OCCUPIED

OCCUPIED

HOW THE HUMAN MIND IS OVERTAKEN WITHOUT RESISTANCE

JACKLEINE SPRING

Published by Solid Ground House Publishing™
Printed in the United States of America
Henderson, Nevada
SolidGroundHousePublishing.com

Library of Congress Cataloging-in- Publication Data

Names: Spring, Jackleine

Title: OCCUPIED: HOW THE HUMAN MIND IS OVERTAKEN WITHOUT RESISTANCE / Jackleine Spring

Description: First Edition | Nevada: Solid Ground House Publishing

Identifiers: LCCN 2026900214
ISBN (soft cover) 979-8-9990232-5-4
ISBN (hard cover) 979-8-9990232-4-7
ISBN (ebook) 979-8-9990232-6-1
ISBN (dust jacket) 979-8-9990232-7-8

Subject: Human agency—Psychological aspects. | Self—Psychology. | Social influence.

CONTENTS

PART 1
THE UNSEEN SHIFT

1

PART 2
Conditions for takeover

23

PART 3
WHY MODERN EXPLANATIONS FAIL

47

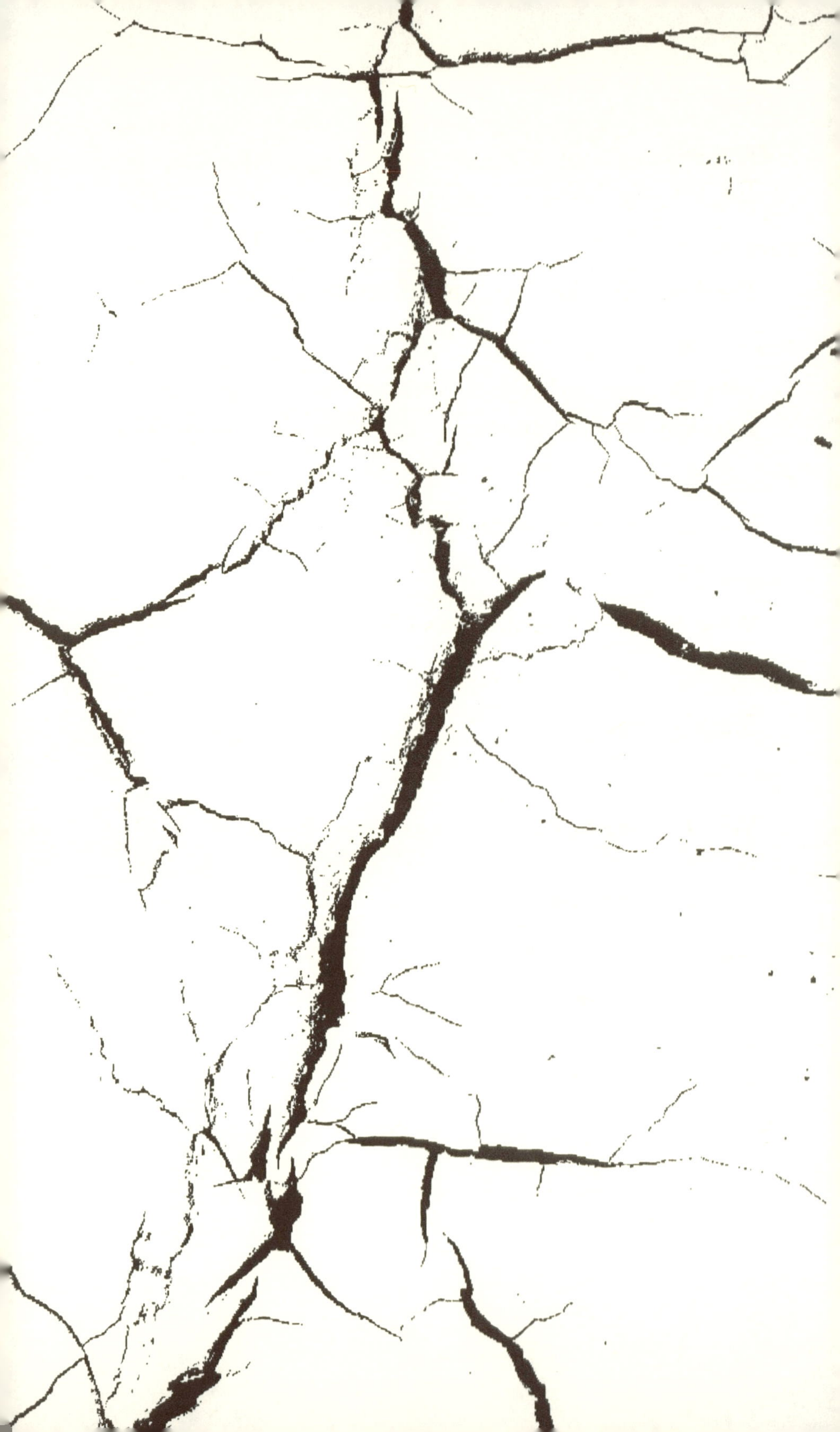

AUTHOR'S NOTE

I did not set out to write this book. I didn't begin with a theory, a message, or a desire to persuade. What I began with was a pattern—one I kept encountering in conversations, in people who appeared functional but inwardly divided, and eventually in my own life.

Again and again, I heard the same language from people who had never compared notes: "I know better, but I can't stop." "I feel like I'm not in charge anymore." "It's like something is pushing me." These were not careless people. They were thoughtful, reflective, often disciplined individuals who had tried everything modern life offers—therapy, insight, self-improvement, spirituality, medication, meaning-making. None of these brought relief. None of them resolved what was happening.

What disturbed me was not the struggle itself. It was the loss of agency—and how little language we have left to talk about it honestly.

This book was written slowly, carefully, and with restraint because the subject demands it. Sensationalism would have been easier. Religious jargon would have been safer. I chose neither. Instead, I chose to follow the experience to its conclusion—even when that conclusion is uncomfortable in modern culture.

I am not interested in fear. I am not interested in control. I am not interested in emotional manipulation. I am interested in truth—and in freedom that actually lasts.

INTRODUCTION

Something has shifted inside a growing number of people. They do not feel like themselves anymore. They function. They work, speak, scroll, socialize, and sleep. From the outside, nothing appears broken. And yet beneath the surface is a persistent sense of foreignness—a feeling that something else has taken up residence in the mind.

They struggle to describe it. "I don't recognize my reactions." "My thoughts feel hostile." "I know what's right, but I can't do it." "It's like something pushes me in the wrong direction." These are not people having a bad week. They are not confused, unintelligent, or disconnected from reality. Many are reflective, self-aware, and actively seeking help. They read. They journal. They attend therapy. They meditate. They try supplements, programs, and protocols. Some improve temporarily. Many do not.

What remains is the same quiet question, returned to again and again: Why do I feel overridden?

Agency is the ability to choose—to restrain, redirect, and govern one's own inner world. It is not happiness. It is not motivation. It is not success. It is the stabilizing sense that you are the one deciding what happens inside you.

When agency weakens, strange things occur. People act against their own values. They sabotage what they love. They resist clarity while claiming to want it. They feel drawn toward what harms them. The most disturbing part is not the behavior itself—it is the absence of resistance. The inner "no" that should arise simply doesn't.

This is often mistaken for weakness or pathology. But many who experience it were once disciplined, thoughtful, and grounded. The change is not gradual character development. It is displacement.

Western culture excels at categorization. We classify symptoms, label disorders, and assign treatments. But in the process, we have excluded an entire category of human experience—not because it was disproven, but because it became uncomfortable.

That category is intrusion.

Not every destructive inner influence originates from the self. Not every voice in the mind belongs to the person hearing it. Across cultures and centuries, this distinction was intuitively understood. Today, it is dismissed reflexively.

As a result, people are taught to negotiate with forces that do not negotiate, to reason with impulses that do not reason, to integrate what is actively dismantling them. And when it fails, they blame themselves.

This is not a book about horror, superstition, or religious spectacle. It is not an argument against psychology, nor a denial of trauma, biology, or emotional pain. These are real and meaningful dimensions of the human experience. But they are not the whole picture.

This book asks a question most people are afraid to ask—even when they feel the answer pressing in from all sides: What if something else is involved? Not metaphorically. Not symbolically. But practically, personally, and measurably.

If possession exists today, it does not announce itself. It does not spin heads or shout obscenities. It dulls. Distracts. Fragments. It replaces conviction with confusion. It trades authority for impulse. Most importantly, it convinces the person it inhabits that nothing is wrong—or that whatever is wrong is their fault.

This is not dramatic. It is efficient. And it thrives in a culture that has lost the ability to say no—internally or externally.

This book does not ask for belief. It asks for honesty. It traces patterns—psychological, behavioral, emotional—that repeat across individuals who feel displaced within themselves. It examines where modern explanations help, where they fail, and what they refuse to consider.

Most of all, it restores a concept that has quietly vanished from modern life: the idea that the self can be invaded—and that invasion can be resisted.

There is a way back to clarity. There is a way back to authority. There is a way back to yourself.

But first, the problem has to be named.

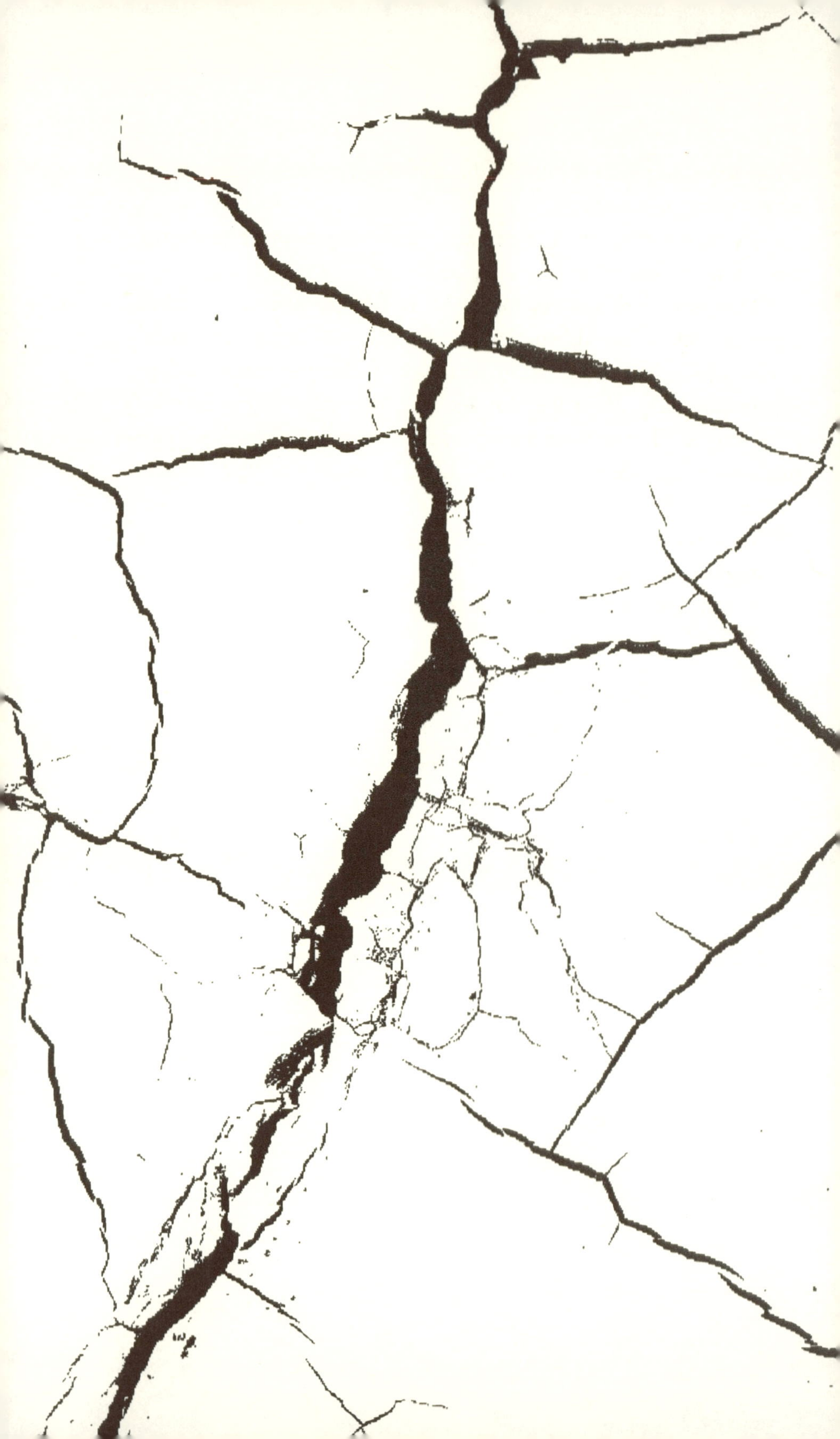

PART 1

THE UNSEEN SHIFT

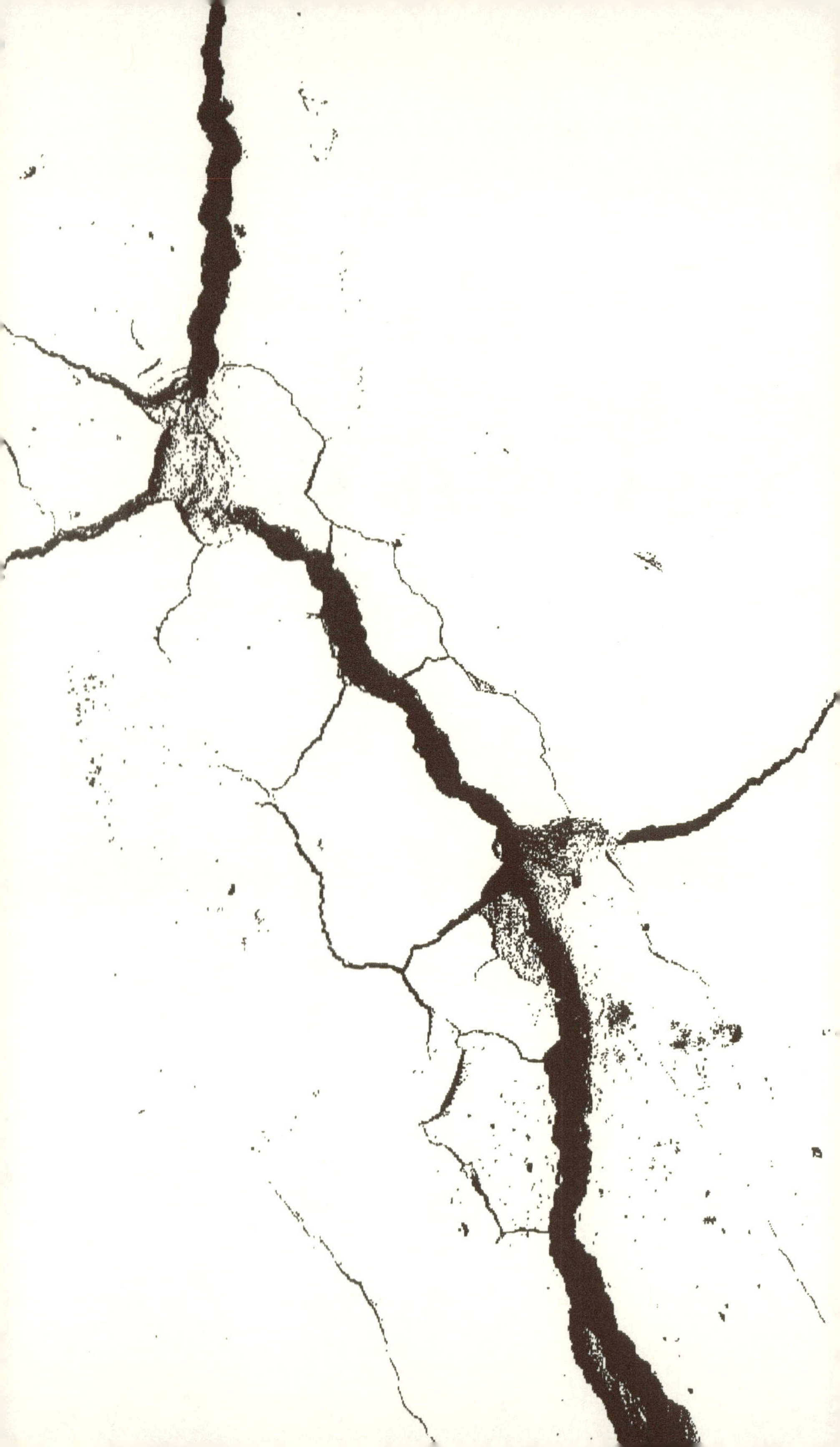

1

WHEN THE SELF IS NO LONGER IN CHARGE

There is a moment many people can recall, even if they never say it aloud. It is the moment they realize their inner world no longer responds to command. They still know what they should do. They can articulate it clearly and explain why it matters. And yet, when the moment arrives, the will to act does not engage. The decision stalls. Thought does not become motion.

This is not laziness, confusion, or ignorance. It is interference. That distinction matters more than it first appears.

Most modern explanations collapse all inner struggle into a single word: motivation. If you fail to act, you are told you do not want it badly enough—or that fear, trauma, or habit is blocking you. But there is a difference between wanting something, knowing something, and being able to choose something. The failure is not always desire or understanding. The third is often missing.

People describe this absence in strikingly similar ways. They say, "It's like something shuts me down." "I feel pulled in the wrong direction." "I argue with myself and lose." "I watch myself do it." The common thread is not emotion. It is the loss of command.

To understand how this happens, the inner order itself has to be examined. A healthy inner world has structure: thoughts arise, judgment evaluates them, and will directs action. When this order is intact, even strong emotions do not dictate behavior. A person can feel anger without acting violently, desire without compulsion, and fear without paralysis.

When the structure erodes, the hierarchy collapses. Impulses outrun judgment. Reactions bypass evaluation. The will becomes a bystander. What replaces it is not chaos, but something more efficient.

The shift is felt long before it is understood. People often describe this stage with shame, assuming it reflects weakness or moral failure. But the language they use reveals something else. They say, "I don't know why I did that." "That wasn't me." "I felt hijacked." "It was like watching myself." These are not metaphors. They are observations.

Something other than the self is exerting influence over action.

Psychology is valuable. It explains patterns, histories, and mechanisms. But explanation is not restoration. Many people who experience this loss of command understand their trauma, recognize their triggers, and can predict their behavior. And yet knowledge does not return authority. They know they commit the act, but do not know why—or how to stop.

This gap is where most frameworks fall silent.

What follows is not theory, but pattern. The most dangerous form of takeover is not forceful. It is gradual. The person still uses their own voice, memories, and personality. Nothing dramatic occurs. Conscience remains intact, and that is why shame grows. Resistance fades, values are violated, and self-respect erodes.

The individual becomes less recognizable—to others, and eventually to themselves. Because the transition is subtle, it is rarely confronted.

One of the clearest signs of interference is the emotional reaction to resistance itself. Clarity feels exhausting. Discipline feels abrasive. Stillness feels threatening. Practices that once grounded the person—reflection, truth-telling, restraint—begin to provoke an inner pushback that feels disproportionate and angry. This is not indifference. It is opposition.

And when opposition cannot be explained, it is usually internalized. When no framework exists to explain the experience, people turn inward. They call themselves broken, weak, disordered, unhealed. Self-blame becomes the default explanation.

But blaming the self for losing command assumes the self is still in charge. That assumption may be wrong.

This chapter is not meant to persuade. It is meant to clarify. This is not a question of belief, but recognition. If you have ever felt overridden, divided, compelled, or resistant to your own healing, then one question deserves serious consideration: what if the struggle is not entirely internal?

Before any solution can be considered, the problem must be seen clearly. The next chapter examines how the inner world becomes vulnerable in the first place—and why modern life creates ideal conditions for intrusion.

2

WHEN YOUR THOUGHTS DON'T FEEL LIKE YOURS

Most people assume their thoughts belong to them. They may not like every thought they have, and they may struggle with negativity, worry, or self-criticism. Still, there is an underlying assumption that remains largely unquestioned: this is my mind. These thoughts originate within me, even if I wish they would stop.

For some, that assumption quietly collapses. The thoughts no longer feel self-generated. They feel imposed—arriving with a force, repetition, or hostility that does not match the person's character or values. They do not respond to reason, soften with insight, or fade with time. Instead, they persist, unmoved by understanding or effort.

This difference is often minimized, but it should not be. Intrusive thoughts are frequently described in clinical language as random or meaningless mental noise—something to be dismissed, reframed, or ignored. But those who experience them know the problem is not their presence alone. It is their quality.

They arrive suddenly and uninvited, repeat with unnatural persistence, and target what the person values most. They feel antagonistic rather than neutral and do not resemble background chatter. They register as pressure, and pressure implies direction.

A particularly disturbing feature many people report is hostility. The thoughts are not merely anxious or pessimistic. They are contemptuous, accusatory, and degrading. They speak in absolutes and finalities, attacking identity rather than circumstance. This voice does not reason, console, or seek understanding. It seeks collapse. The most unsettling part is not what it says, but how foreign it feels to the person hearing it.

Most people attempt to deal with intrusive thoughts through logic or reframing. They challenge them, analyze them, and trace them back to childhood, trauma, or insecurity. Sometimes this helps. But many find that the thoughts adapt. They counter the counterargument, grow louder when resisted, and return stronger after moments of clarity. The effort to reclaim the mind seems to provoke escalation rather than relief.

At that point, the issue is no longer content. It is authority.

Modern frameworks often treat the mind as a collection of equal voices—parts to be integrated, welcomed, or negotiated with. But the lived experience of those affected contradicts this model. These thoughts do not behave like wounded parts seeking healing. They do not soften when acknowledged or integrate when welcomed. They dominate.

Because people sense this difference, they often struggle to describe the experience without sounding irrational. Many also report something harder to explain: the sense that speaking plainly about it is not allowed. As a result, they soften their language, even to themselves. They describe the experience as invasive, as though their mind is no longer private, as though they cannot keep things out, as though there is no off switch.

What they are describing is not distraction. It is trespass. A boundary that once existed no longer holds.

One of the most dangerous aspects of intrusive thought is how effectively it turns the person against themselves. It isolates, erodes trust in one's own perception, and undermines confidence in judgment. Over time, the person begins to doubt not only their thoughts, but their right to think clearly at all. This is how agency erodes at the mental level.

Before behavior changes, before values invert, before identity shifts, the takeover begins in thought.

This matters because behavior is visible, while thought is not. A person can appear functional while their inner world is under siege. They may maintain responsibilities, relationships, and appearances while internally navigating relentless pressure. This is why the problem is so often missed. There is no spectacle, no crisis, and no obvious breakdown—only a steady erosion of mental sovereignty.

Every healthy mind requires a boundary. Not every thought deserves consideration, not every impulse deserves attention, and not every voice deserves a hearing. When a person loses the ability to distinguish what arises from what belongs, they lose more than peace. They lose ownership.

This chapter does not attempt to explain why these thoughts arrive. It establishes something more basic: that the experience itself is real, that it follows a pattern, and that dismissing it as meaningless noise fails the people living inside it.

The next chapter examines what happens when this loss of mental ownership spreads beyond thought—into conscience, restraint, and moral clarity. When the mind can no longer say no, the rest of the self soon follows.

3

THE DISAPPEARANCE OF THE INNER AUTHORITY

Long before behavior collapses, something quieter disappears. It is not intelligence, awareness, or even morality. It is authority—the inner capacity to say no and have that no mean something.

Most people assume authority is external: laws, rules, expectations, consequences. But the most important form of authority is internal. It is the ability to govern oneself even when no one is watching, no pressure is applied, and no reward is offered. When this authority is intact, a person may struggle, but they are not ruled. When it erodes, the self loses its command center.

Inner authority is often confused with discipline or willpower, but it is neither. Discipline is behavioral. Willpower is effort-based. Authority is structural. It is the organizing principle that determines which thoughts are entertained, which impulses are resisted, and which actions are permitted. A person with inner authority can feel strong emotion without obeying it, experience desire without surrendering to it, and hear an inner argument without submitting to it. Authority does not require force. It requires position.

The disappearance of inner authority is rarely dramatic. There is no moment of collapse, no internal announcement, no sudden loss of function. Instead, there are small concessions. A thought that would once have been dismissed is allowed to linger. An impulse that would have been restrained is entertained. A boundary that would have been upheld is postponed. Nothing feels catastrophic. Each moment appears justified, understandable, even compassionate. Authority does not vanish all at once. Its absence is revealed through repetition.

Judgment remains intact, but it no longer carries force. Each repetition confirms the same discovery: action proceeds without authorization.

What repeats is not choice but execution, until the loss of authority becomes undeniable. A person can recognize a behavior as harmful and still feel powerless to stop it. They can see consequences clearly and yet feel unable to alter course. Judgment becomes commentary rather than command, creating a demoralizing state in which the self knows but cannot intervene. Over time, knowing without power breeds resignation.

One of the clearest signs authority has eroded is the shift in how people relate to their own impulses. Instead of directing them, they begin negotiating. They bargain, compromise, and postpone resistance. "I'll stop tomorrow." "Just this once." "It's not that bad." This language reflects a change in position. The self is no longer leading; it is pleading. Once pleading becomes normal, the decline accelerates.

Modern culture often associates authority with oppression. Control is framed as repression. Boundaries are framed as denial. Restraint is framed as harm. As a result, people are encouraged to treat every inner impulse as meaningful, every desire as authentic, and every resistance as suspicious. But authority is not tyranny. It is protection. When protection is reframed as violence, the self is left undefended.

When authority recedes, something else fills the space. Not neutrality. Not freedom. Power vacuums do not remain empty. Impulses grow louder. Thoughts become more insistent. Reactions accelerate. What once required effort now happens automatically. The person feels increasingly carried rather than choosing, moved by internal forces they no longer command.

This is why shame often intensifies as authority decreases. It seems counterintuitive—if a person feels less in control, why would self-condemnation grow? Because the conscience remains while the capacity to act on it fades. The person still knows what is right; they simply cannot enforce it. This mismatch produces chronic self-accusation without resolution. The result is not moral clarity but exhaustion.

At this stage, many people unknowingly make a trade. They surrender authority in exchange for relief. If resisting feels impossible, surrender feels merciful. If self-command feels hostile, passivity feels kind. But relief gained through abdication is temporary. What is surrendered does not remain unused, and this is where something more disorienting begins to appear.

There are people living lives they would not have chosen if they had been fully present when the choices were made. They wake up one day and realize they are saying things they do not believe, doing things they once judged, tolerating behaviors they once swore they never would. What unsettles them most is not that they changed, but that they do not remember deciding to.

They still recognize themselves internally. Their values are intact. Their conscience still reacts. But their behavior no longer matches their inner life. They hear themselves agree when they do not agree. They stay silent when resistance rises. They participate in things that feel wrong—not dramatically wrong, but quietly misaligned. Later, when alone, the thought appears: Why did I do that? That isn't me.

This is not hypocrisy. Hypocrisy requires intention. This does not. What is happening is more disturbing: they are living out a version of themselves they did not author. The lie is not spoken outwardly at first. It is lived.

A man finds himself numb in a career he once despised, repeating language he does not respect, defending decisions he knows are hollow. A woman hears herself laughing at things that offend her spirit, reshaping her boundaries to fit a world she no longer recognizes. Someone compromises again, telling themselves it is temporary, until the temporary becomes permanent.

When they try to explain it, the words do not come. They do not feel possessed. They feel confused. They still know who they are; they just do not know how they got so far from it. This is one of the most dangerous forms of occupation—not when awareness is lost, but when awareness remains while control quietly disappears.

Now tension develops inside the self. The conscience protests while the body complies. The inner voice reacts, but over time it grows quieter—not because it stopped speaking, but because it learned it would not be obeyed.

In some cases, this quieting is not the end of the process. There are moments when a thought begins to form—not an ordinary thought, but one that would interrupt the pattern and reassert authority. Before it can complete itself, it is taken away. The interruption is immediate. The moment the direction of thought turns toward resistance, the inner process halts. The sentence dissolves before it can finish. The mind does not argue with the thought; it removes it.

What follows is not confusion but muteness. The person does not lose the ability to think in general. They can still reason, speak, and function. But the specific line of thought that would lead toward freedom cannot be held. It disappears the moment it begins to organize. The person senses this happening. They recognize the direction the thought was taking. They know it mattered. When they try to return to it, there is nothing there.

This is why, when confronted, no words come out—not because the person refuses to speak or fears saying the wrong thing, but because the access point to that inner material has been shut down. The mouth opens, but the thought that should supply the words has already been removed.

This creates a specific form of immobilization. The self can observe what is happening. The conscience can still react. But the moment where interruption would occur—the moment where the self would speak, name, or resist—never completes. This is not blankness. It is interception. Once this becomes consistent, the person stops expecting interruption to be possible at all, not because they surrendered, but because every attempt to form it was ended before it could exist.

This is how people end up defending what they once resisted, justifying what they once rejected, and living lies they never consciously chose—not because they wanted to become someone else, but because they stopped interrupting the drift.

Across individuals who experience this erosion, the pattern is consistent. Inner resistance weakens. Impulses gain momentum. Judgment loses force. Self-trust erodes. The person does not become chaotic. They become directed—but not by themselves.

This chapter does not argue that inner authority disappears on its own. It raises a simpler, more unsettling question: if authority has withdrawn, what has taken its place?

Before that question can be answered, something else must be examined. The next chapter looks at how identity itself begins to shift—sometimes subtly, sometimes suddenly—once inner authority is no longer in control. Because when the one who should lead steps aside, something else inevitably steps forward.

4

PERSONALITY DRIFT AND SUDDEN INVERSION

The loss of inner authority does not stay contained. Once command weakens, it begins to affect not just behavior but character. People often recognize this only in hindsight. Looking back, they can identify a period where something began to feel off—not situationally, but personally. They were still themselves in name, memory, and appearance, yet their responses no longer matched who they believed themselves to be.

This is not growth. It is not maturation or evolution. It is drift. Healthy change feels intentional. Even when difficult, it carries a sense of alignment—a recognition that the person is becoming more themselves, not less. Personality drift feels different. The changes arrive without consent. They are not the result of reflection or decision. They feel imposed, almost accidental.

People describe it in similar terms. They say they do not know when they became like this, that they would not have reacted this way before, that this is not how they used to think, that they no longer recognize themselves. The unsettling feature is not the change itself. It is the absence of authorship.

In some cases, the shift is subtle and gradual. In others, it is abrupt. Values once held firmly begin to reverse. Habits once resisted become routine. Lines once considered non-negotiable begin to blur or disappear entirely. What was once repellent becomes tolerable. What was once important becomes irritating. What was once loved becomes burdensome.

This is not moral complexity. It is inversion.

Life changes people. Stress reshapes priorities. Pain hardens or softens us in different ways. Not every shift in personality is concerning. What distinguishes inversion is direction. The changes consistently move away from restraint, truthfulness, responsibility, and integration, and toward impulsivity, distortion, fragmentation, and self-erasure. Adaptation aims toward survival or coherence. Inversion undermines both.

One of the earliest signs of this process is inconsistency—not occasional contradiction, which is human, but a deeper loss of continuity. People begin acting in ways that contradict their own stated beliefs, then defending those actions with explanations that feel hollow even to themselves. They say that this is just who they are now, that people change, that they are done caring. The tone is not conviction. It is resignation.

Another common feature of personality drift is the erosion of empathy. This does not always appear as cruelty. More often, it appears as indifference. Concern for others feels inconvenient. Responsibility feels intrusive. Commitment feels like a threat. People do not necessarily become malicious. They become disengaged, and disengagement makes harm easier.

As personality shifts, defensiveness often increases. Questions feel like attacks. Concern feels like control. Accountability feels hostile. This defensiveness serves a purpose. It prevents interruption. The more the drift progresses, the more fiercely it resists examination—not because the person is unaware, but because something in them does not want to be seen clearly.

Earlier chapters explored the phrase "that wasn't me." Here, it takes on a darker meaning. At first, it expresses confusion. Later, it becomes grief. People begin mourning a version of themselves they can no longer access, while simultaneously acting in ways that further distance them from that self. This internal contradiction produces numbness. Feeling becomes dangerous. Reflection becomes painful. The self retreats further.

Often, friends or family recognize the shift before the individual does. They sense increased irritability, reduced accountability, moral inconsistency, and emotional withdrawal. But raising these concerns rarely helps. When confronted, speech often collapses. Words fail to form. Thought does not organize. There is no defense—only confusion, evasion, or denial that anything is happening at all.

The reality cannot be confronted aloud. It is not argued against. It is simply unspeakable.

Left unexamined, personality drift solidifies. What begins as deviation becomes identity. What begins as impulse becomes repetition, even as conscience protests. What begins as erosion becomes normal. At this stage, people often insist they are finally being authentic. But authenticity that destroys coherence is not authenticity. It is surrender.

There is a difference between changing and being changed. One preserves authorship. The other replaces it.

This chapter does not claim that every personality shift signals external influence. It establishes something simpler and more unsettling. When identity changes in a direction that consistently undermines clarity, restraint, and wholeness, and does so without consent, authorship must be questioned.

One of the ways authorship is lost is through the quiet discrediting of resistance. At first, resistance feels like clarity—a tightening in the chest, a hesitation before agreeing, a quiet sense that something is not right. People notice it and ignore it. They tell themselves they are overthinking, too sensitive, out of step. The resistance does not disappear. It returns again and again, each time slightly weaker, not because it is wrong, but because it has been overridden.

Eventually, something subtle changes. People stop interpreting resistance as information and begin treating it as interference. They feel the inner pause and push past it automatically. They sense hesitation and override it with logic. They dismiss discomfort before it finishes forming. They stop asking why they feel resistance and start asking how to get rid of it.

This is a quiet turning point. Resistance was never the problem. It was the signal. Once people stop trusting it, they no longer have an internal braking system. They move faster, agree more easily, and commit with less reflection. When things feel wrong afterward, they blame themselves rather than the decision. They tell themselves they should be more adaptable, that they need to stop being difficult, that this is just how life works. What they do not say is that something in them knew better.

Over time, resistance stops showing up altogether—not because it was invalid, but because it learned it would not be honored. This is one of the most effective stages of occupation. The self does not need to be silenced. It only needs to be discredited.

Once people stop trusting their own internal warning system, they can be led anywhere—willingly, calmly, efficiently. They do not feel controlled. They feel reasonable. And that is when the self is no longer in charge.

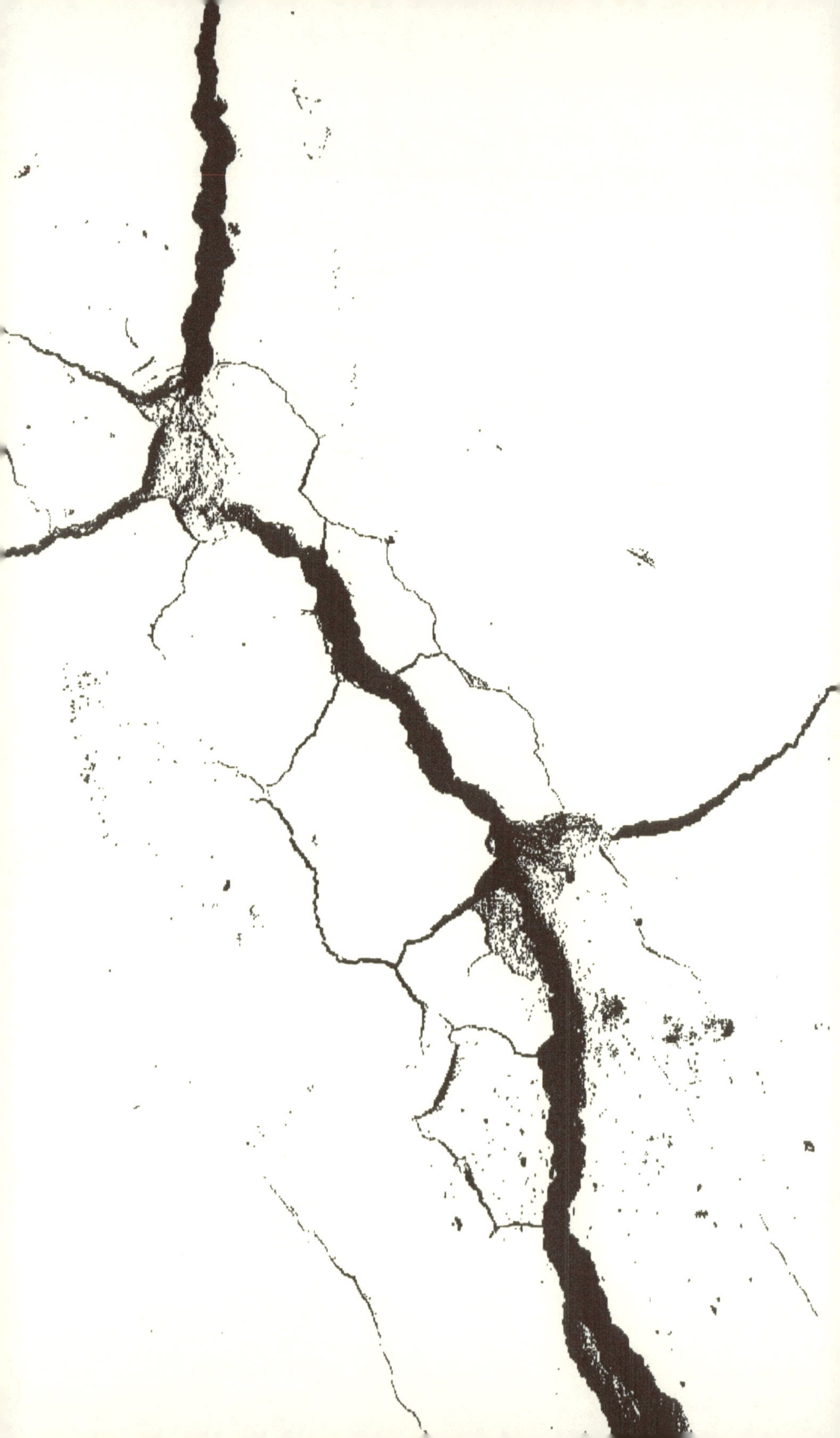

PART 2

CONDITIONS FOR TAKEOVER

5

FRAGMENTATION: A DIVIDED INNER WORLD

A unified self is difficult to displace. As long as thought, conscience, memory, and will remain connected, outside influence struggles to gain traction. Even intense pressure meets resistance, and even strong impulses encounter limits. Fragmentation changes that.

Fragmentation does not mean multiple personalities or overt psychological collapse. It is quieter and far more common. It is the splitting of the inner world into compartments that no longer communicate or answer to a single authority. The self becomes divided, not destroyed, and division makes intrusion easier.

Fragmentation occurs when parts of the inner life operate independently rather than coherently. Thought detaches from action. Emotion detaches from meaning. Memory detaches from responsibility. Desire detaches from consequence. The person still functions, and often functions well, but beneath the surface the self is no longer unified. Instead of one center, there are many, and none fully govern the others.

Fragmentation rarely begins as a choice. It starts as a coping strategy. When pain feels overwhelming, the mind learns to separate. When attention is overloaded, it learns to scatter. When life demands constant response, it learns to stay shallow. Disconnection becomes adaptive at first. It allows survival and reduces intensity. But what protects in crisis can weaken in stability. Over time, the habit of separation becomes the default state.

Trauma is a well-known cause of fragmentation, and rightly so. Severe or prolonged stress can fracture the inner world as a means of self-preservation. But fragmentation also emerges from conditions that appear ordinary. Constant digital stimulation, chronic distraction, sleep deprivation, emotional suppression, perpetual urgency, and identity performance may not seem dangerous in isolation. Together, they produce a mind that never fully arrives anywhere.

When the self is fragmented, awareness becomes inconsistent. A person may feel remorse in one moment and indifference the next. They may understand consequences intellectually while remaining emotionally detached. They may hold values sincerely yet violate them repeatedly. This inconsistency is not hypocrisy. It is disconnection. The parts that know are no longer linked to the parts that act.

A unified self can resist. A fragmented self negotiates. Each part experiences pressure separately. One part feels guilt. Another seeks relief. Another rationalizes. Another disengages entirely. There is no central authority to arbitrate. Resistance dissolves not through force, but through diffusion.

One of the most significant casualties of fragmentation is the loss of the inner witness—the capacity to observe oneself as a whole. Without it, behavior happens without reflection, decisions occur without integration, and consequences register late, if at all. The person lives in moments rather than continuity, and without continuity, accountability fades.

Modern life quietly rewards fragmentation. Multitasking is praised. Distraction is monetized. Emotional numbing is normalized. Constant input is expected. A fragmented mind is easier to occupy with information, influence, impulse, and noise. Stillness becomes unfamiliar. Silence becomes uncomfortable. Presence feels unsafe. These are not personal failures. They are environmental conditions.

A divided inner world is not empty, but it is open. When no single authority governs thought, emotion, and action, influence does not need to conquer. It only needs access. This is why fragmentation so reliably precedes takeover. It creates internal gaps—spaces where direction can enter without resistance.

As fragmentation deepens, attempts at reintegration often provoke discomfort. Slowing down feels agitating. Reflection feels heavy. Clarity feels destabilizing. People often interpret this as proof they are not ready to heal. But the resistance itself is informative. What resists reintegration does not benefit from wholeness.

Fragmentation is not possession, but it prepares the ground. It weakens coherence, dissolves command, and removes the unified no. A fragmented self is not powerless, but it is vulnerable.

At some point, people stop living their lives and begin maintaining them. They no longer wake up asking what they believe or want. They wake up asking what is required to keep everything running—the job, the image, the relationships, the version of themselves others expect. Slowly, often without realizing it, they begin to perform.

They say the right things, react the right way, and hold the correct opinions at the correct volume. Not because they are fake, but because authenticity has become inconvenient. What is unsettling is how natural this starts to feel. They do not feel like liars. They feel tired—tired of explaining, tired of resisting, tired of being the friction in the room.

So they become agreeable, adaptable, and low-resistance. They smooth themselves out. The longer this continues, the harder it becomes to tell where the performance ends and the person begins. They still have moments of clarity—brief flashes where something inside stiffens and signals that something is not right. But those moments pass. They are inconvenient, and the performance is rewarded.

The world responds positively to the version of them that asks no questions, interrupts nothing, and challenges no direction. So they continue, not because they believe in the life they are living, but because stopping would require confrontation—with others, with consequences, and with themselves.

Over time, something subtle shifts. They stop asking who they are and start asking who they need to be today. That is the moment the self is no longer leading.

The self is not overtaken by force or erased. It is quietly replaced by a role that receives approval. There is a stage where compliance begins to feel like calm. The inner conflict quiets. Resistance fades. Friction disappears. People mistake the absence of tension for peace. They tell themselves they have grown, matured, or learned to let things go.

But peace does not come from surrendering the self. Peace comes from alignment. What they are experiencing is not rest. It is shutdown. The nervous system settles because it no longer has to fight. The conscience quiets because it no longer expects to be obeyed. The self steps back because insisting has proven costly.

This creates a deceptive sense of relief. Life feels smoother, less demanding, and easier to manage. Because nothing is actively hurting, people assume something has healed. But healing restores capacity. This removes it. They stop objecting not because things are right, but because objection no longer changes outcomes. They stop pushing not because they agree, but because pushing requires strength they no longer feel authorized to use.

This is how obedience becomes mislabeled as peace. It looks composed, responsible, even virtuous. But underneath it is resignation. True peace does not require the self to disappear. It does not demand silence or ask the will to step aside. When peace is real, the self remains present.

When obedience replaces peace, the self recedes, and the absence is mistaken for growth. This is one of the most effective disguises occupation uses, because people stop resisting not when they are defeated, but when they believe they have arrived.

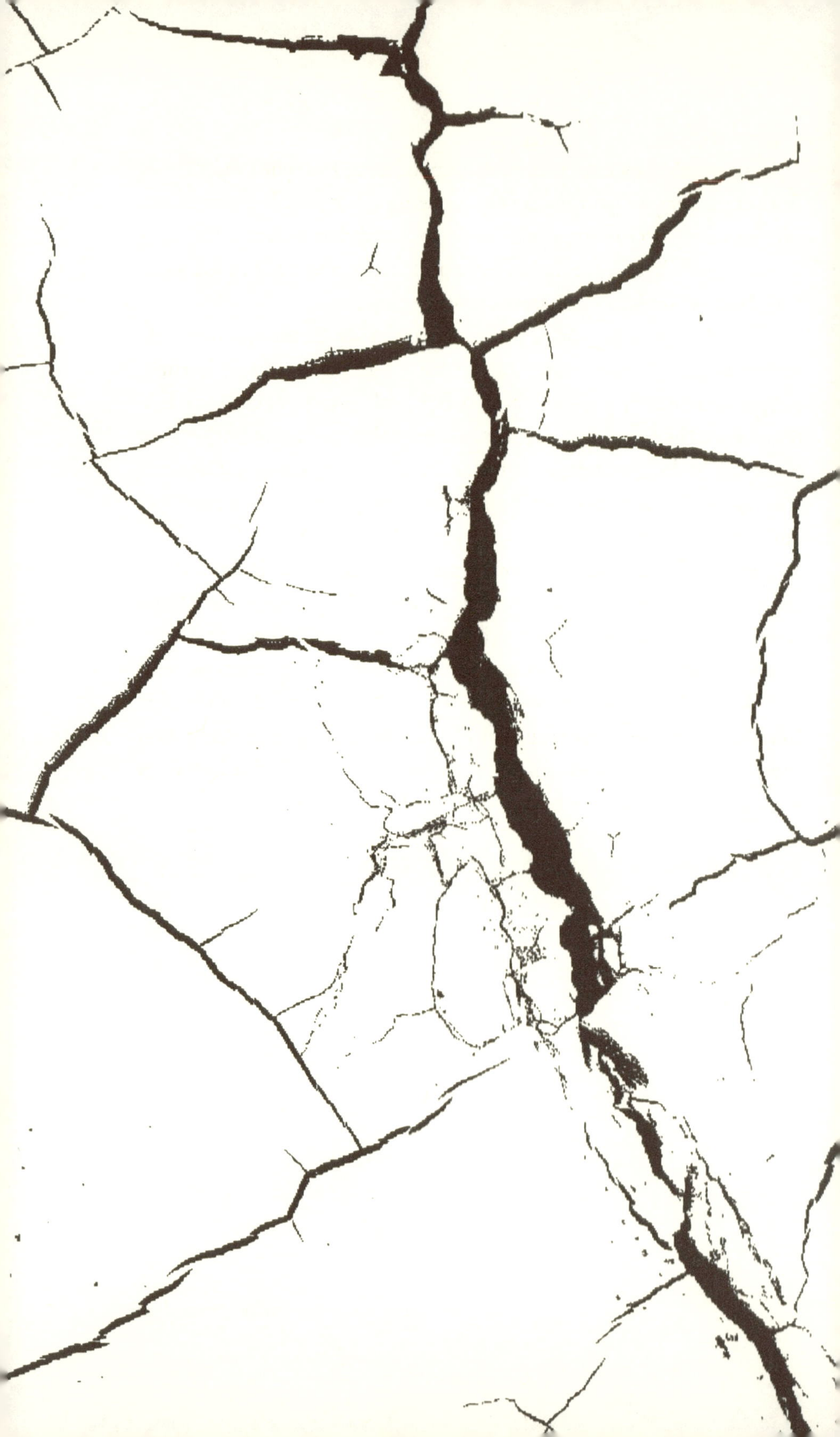

6

NUMBNESS AS AN OPEN DOOR

Numbness is often mistaken for peace. When pain overwhelms, emotional flattening can feel like relief. When anxiety burns too hot, detachment feels like control. When life becomes too loud, too fast, too demanding, the absence of feeling can seem merciful. But numbness is not neutral. It is not rest, healing, or stability. It is a vacancy.

Most people do not choose numbness directly. They choose survival. They stop reacting because reacting hurts. They stop caring because caring costs too much. They stop feeling because feeling no longer feels safe. At first, this appears adaptive. The edges soften. The intensity drops. The pressure eases. But something essential is lost along with the pain.

Emotion is not merely sensation. It is information. It alerts, warns, and signals alignment or danger. When numbness sets in, these signals dim. Guilt fades. Joy dulls. Concern weakens. Aversion quiets. The inner alarm system goes offline, and without alarm, intrusion encounters less resistance.

Numbness creates space—not empty space, but unguarded space. When feeling recedes, something else gains room to operate. Impulses no longer meet emotional friction. Thoughts move without resonance. Actions occur without internal consequence. The person feels less, but they are not freer. They are less anchored.

One of the most overlooked indicators of vulnerability is indifference. Not anger. Not despair. But apathy. People stop caring about things they once protected. Truth, integrity, responsibility, and relationship are no longer defended, even though they are still recognized as important. They say it does not matter, that they are tired of caring, that they just want peace. But peace obtained through disengagement is not peace. It is retreat.

Pain provokes resistance. Numbness does not. A person in pain still pushes back. A numb person stops pushing altogether. This is why numbness is so useful to forces that seek access. There is no argument to win, no boundary to breach, no defense to overcome. The door is already open.

Modern culture quietly rewards emotional flattening. Feel less. React less. Care selectively. Constant stimulation dulls sensitivity. Endless outrage exhausts discernment. Chronic exposure numbs response. Over time, the absence of feeling is reframed as maturity. People are told they are detached now, that they are protecting their energy, that they have evolved. But detachment without authority is not evolution. It is exposure.

One of the most dangerous effects of numbness is the erosion of moral sensation. Right and wrong begin to feel abstract. Consequences feel distant. Values feel negotiable. The person may still believe in goodness, but no longer feel compelled by it. This is not moral failure. It is sensory loss.

Suppressed feeling does not disappear. It relocates. What is not felt consciously often returns as impulse, compulsion, or agitation. The person who feels nothing suddenly acts without understanding why. The numbness breaks briefly, but only in behavior. This creates confusion. If nothing is felt, why does action still occur? Because numbness does not remove influence. It removes awareness.

Numbness promises rest without restoration. It offers relief without repair. And it asks for something in return: alertness, sensitivity, and discernment. What is given up is not pain alone. It is protection. Numbness is not possession, but it lowers resistance. It silences warning systems, dulls internal boundaries, and makes intrusion efficient.

A person does not need to be overwhelmed to be overtaken. They only need to stop feeling enough to notice.

At some point, people stop questioning their lives and start defending them—not because the questions were answered, but because the questions became dangerous. At first, the doubts were quiet: a discomfort late at night, a sense that something did not fit the person they believed themselves to be. Over time, those doubts threatened stability.

Questioning the job meant questioning the years already invested. Questioning the relationship meant confronting what staying had cost. Questioning the life meant admitting it was not freely chosen. So the questions were replaced, not with truth, but with justification. People begin explaining their lives instead of examining them. They rehearse reasons instead of listening to resistance.

They say that this is just how things are, that nothing is perfect, that it could be worse. They defend choices they no longer feel aligned with, not because they believe in them, but because letting go would require upheaval. What is unsettling is how convincing the defense becomes. They sound confident, certain, resolved. But beneath the words is tension.

Defending something is different from standing behind it. Defense implies threat. It implies fragility. The harder someone defends their life, the more likely it is that part of them is trying not to see it clearly. This is how occupation deepens. The mind does not need to silence the conscience. It only needs to keep it busy explaining.

For many people, the most frightening thought is not that this is not who they are, but what would happen if they admitted it. Admission threatens structure. It would mean acknowledging wasted time, misplaced loyalty, and years spent maintaining something that quietly eroded the self. That feels unbearable.

So people choose the safer option. They live the lie, not loudly or dramatically, but consistently. They stay in situations that drain them. They continue paths that feel hollow. They accept a version of themselves that feels diminished, not because they are unaware, but because awareness without action feels destabilizing.

There is a particular exhaustion that comes from knowing your life is misaligned and continuing anyway. It shows up as irritability, numbness, and quiet resentment toward people who live more freely. Instead of confronting the source, people harden around it. They become defensive when the topic arises, dismissive when others question the same things they once questioned, and protective of the very systems that limit them.

If someone else breaks free, it forces a comparison they cannot afford to make. This is how people become guardians of the lives that trapped them, not because they love those lives, but because admitting regret would mean facing grief they do not know how to carry.

Eventually, feeling becomes too costly. The mind can only hold so much tension between what it knows and what it continues to do. When awareness does not lead to change, something else steps in to keep the system running. That something is numbness—not dramatic emptiness or despair, but a quiet dulling.

People stop reacting the way they used to. Things that once disturbed them barely register. Choices that once felt heavy now feel procedural. They do not tell themselves they have changed. They tell themselves they are coping. They say they are tired, burned out, overstimulated. That is true, but incomplete.

What is really happening is that the self has learned that feeling without action is intolerable. So it reduces the feeling. This numbness is not a failure. It is an adaptation. It allows people to continue living lives they would otherwise be unable to tolerate.

They stop expecting fulfillment, anticipating joy, or hoping things will feel right again. They lower the bar, not consciously but internally. What once felt wrong now feels distant. What once felt urgent now feels abstract. The ache dulls into background noise, and because there is no acute pain, there is no alarm.

Life continues smoothly. People show up, meet expectations, and fulfill roles. From the outside, everything appears stable. Inside, something essential has gone quiet. Not the conscience, which remains. Not awareness, which is still present. What disappears is urgency.

The self no longer pushes, interrupts, or insists. Numbness becomes the compromise between truth and survival. Once numbness sets in, drift accelerates. When the cost of misalignment is no longer felt, there is nothing left to resist it.

There is a moment that passes almost unnoticed. It is not loud or emotional. It does not announce itself. Something happens that once would have triggered protest, and nothing rises. No hesitation. No discomfort. No internal pause. Just continuation.

People notice it later, in retrospect. They realize something occurred that should have felt wrong, heavy, or at least worth stopping over. But it did not. That absence is unsettling, because objection used to be automatic. The self used to interrupt, question, and slow things down. Now decisions move straight through without resistance.

This is not peace. It is silence. The internal voice has not agreed. It has stepped aside. People do not feel relieved. They feel neutral. They tell themselves they have matured, learned to let things go, and accepted reality. But acceptance still involves awareness. This is something else.

This is quiet resignation, the resolution of inner conflict by removing one side of it. Life becomes smoother, easier to navigate, and less emotionally demanding. Because nothing hurts sharply anymore, nothing demands attention.

This is how occupation completes itself—not when the self disappears, but when nothing inside it objects. When it no longer argues, insists, or interrupts the forward motion of a life it did not choose. From here on, movement does not require consent. The system runs, and the person inside it adjusts.

7

THE HATRED OF STILLNESS

There was a time when stillness was considered restorative. Silence allowed the mind to settle. Solitude clarified thought. Rest revealed what mattered. Stillness was not empty; it was orienting.

For many people now, stillness feels unbearable. Not boring or inconvenient, but actively threatening. When external noise drops away, a strange reaction often appears. People reach for their phone without thinking. They turn on background sound immediately. They feel restless, uneasy, irritated. Silence does not calm them. It provokes them.

The discomfort arrives quickly, sometimes within seconds, and carries a sense of urgency that feels disproportionate to the situation. This is not preference. It is aversion.

Often, the reaction to stillness is physical before it is psychological. There is tightness in the chest, pressure in the head, a surge of nervous energy, and an impulse to move, scroll, speak, or distract. The body responds as if to a threat, even though nothing external is happening. The disturbance originates within.

Stillness removes buffers. It strips away stimulation, narrative, and momentum, leaving the inner world exposed and unmediated by noise. For a unified, grounded person, this exposure brings clarity. For a fragmented or numbed person, it brings confrontation. Thoughts surface. Conflicts emerge. Contradictions become visible. Stillness does not create these things. It reveals them.

When stillness exposes discomfort, the reflex is immediate avoidance. People distract themselves not because they enjoy stimulation, but because they are fleeing something unresolved—guilt, fear, internal hostility, or dissonance they cannot resolve. Distraction becomes not entertainment, but defense.

There is a stage where the problem is no longer what a person thinks, but that they cannot think long enough to form resistance. A thought begins to surface, not a solution, but a recognition that something is wrong or no longer acceptable. Before it can organize, it is gone. It is not replaced by another thought or argued against. It is simply removed.

What follows is not clarity, but blankness. People describe this as freezing, but it is not fear-based paralysis. It is a mental interruption, as if the sentence never finishes forming. They try to explain it to others and find there are no words—not because the experience is irrational, but because language itself will not assemble. The mind spins without content.

This creates a specific kind of isolation. A person may be surrounded by others, function socially, and appear articulate in every other area of life. But when it comes to their inner reality, there is nothing to say—not because nothing is happening, but because the part that could describe it cannot remain active long enough to speak.

This is not avoidance. It is interruption. Once interruption becomes familiar, defense becomes automatic. Once defense becomes habitual, the internal line begins moving without notice.

Most people do not abandon themselves all at once. They cross a line and tell themselves it was just this once. It does not feel dramatic or decisive. It feels temporary. They say something they do not believe to keep the peace. They stay quiet when they should speak to avoid conflict. They agree to something that feels wrong, telling themselves they will correct it later.

Later never comes. Once the line is crossed, it quietly relocates. The second time feels easier. The third time barely registers. Soon, discomfort fades—not because the act became right, but because resistance learned it would not be honored.

What is dangerous is not the first compromise. It is the repetition. Each time the self protests and is ignored, something internal adjusts. The conscience does not disappear; it recalibrates to survive. People do not feel corrupted. They feel adapted.

They tell themselves they are being realistic, flexible, mature. Underneath that language is something truer. They are learning how to live with a version of themselves they do not respect. Eventually, they stop remembering where the original line was, not because their values changed, but because those values were no longer consulted.

This is how people wake up one day shocked by their own tolerance. They look at what they now accept and realize they never would have allowed it before. They are right. But the moment to stop it did not come with a warning label. It came quietly, disguised as convenience.

This is how occupation stabilizes itself, not through force, but through adjustment. The self does not leave. It learns not to interrupt.

Stillness often brings truth to the surface, not abstract truth, but personal truth. Awareness of misalignment emerges. Compromise becomes visible. Memories that were never integrated resurface. Choices that no longer sit quietly demand attention. For someone whose inner authority is weakened, truth feels less like guidance and more like accusation. Rather than orienting the self, it destabilizes it.

This is why truth begins to feel hostile. Many assume they resist stillness because they are restless or overstimulated. But the intensity of the reaction suggests something deeper. The resistance feels emotional. The avoidance feels urgent. The pushback feels angry. This is not neutrality. It is opposition.

A fragmented inner world relies on movement to remain fragmented. Stillness threatens that structure. It allows integration, invites coherence, and restores perspective. For anything that benefits from division, stillness is dangerous. It reduces access.

Modern culture increasingly frames silence as suspicious. People are told they are isolating, overthinking, or in need of stimulation. Stillness is treated as avoidance rather than presence. But constant input does not heal fragmentation. It preserves it.

Underneath the hatred of stillness is often fear—not fear of being alone, but fear of encountering something already present. The person senses that if they stop moving, consuming, and reacting, something will confront them. They may not know what it is, but they know it does not feel safe.

When stillness is avoided long enough, noise becomes necessary. Silence feels wrong. Calm feels suspicious. Order feels oppressive. Chaos becomes familiar, and familiarity is mistaken for comfort. This inversion makes intrusion easier. Noise obscures. Motion distracts. Confusion disorients. Stillness clarifies.

It is not only noisy people who drift. Some of the most captured lives belong to people with good intentions. They believe they are protected because they mean well. They are sincere, thoughtful, and careful. They assume captivity happens only to the reckless or corrupt. But intention does not govern authority, and good motives do not preserve sovereignty.

Most people do not drift because they desire harm. They drift because they are trying to be reasonable. They compromise to keep peace, comply to avoid conflict, and adapt to maintain stability. Each decision feels justified in isolation. They are not abandoning their values. They are postponing them.

Postponement accumulates. Good intentions do not interrupt systems that reward compliance and punish resistance. In fact, they often accelerate capture. Sincere people are more likely to give the benefit of the doubt, absorb discomfort quietly, assume responsibility for problems they did not create, and believe endurance is virtue. This makes them highly adaptable and easily absorbed.

They do not guard the will aggressively. They trust the environment. They assume alignment will return naturally. By the time they realize it has not, the mechanisms required to correct course have already weakened. They still care. They still want what is right. But wanting is no longer enough.

This is why captivity is so often populated by well-intentioned people—not because they lacked values, but because values alone do not preserve agency. Capture does not require malice. It requires time, pressure, and a willingness to endure without insisting.

This chapter does not argue that stillness is always pleasant. It asks a more revealing question: why does the absence of noise feel intolerable? Discomfort with silence is not a flaw. It is a signal.

Fragmentation divides the self. Numbness quiets warning systems. Hatred of stillness prevents reintegration. The next chapter examines what emerges in this environment, when compulsion is mistaken for choice and destruction is defended as freedom. Because when the self can no longer be still, it is easily moved.

8

COMPULSION MASQUERADING AS CHOICE

Few people believe they are being controlled. They believe they are choosing. They insist their actions reflect preference, desire, or freedom, even when those actions repeatedly undermine their health, relationships, values, or future. This is the final illusion.

Choice implies agency. It requires the ability to say yes or no with equal access to both. When one option is inaccessible, when resistance feels impossible, choice becomes a performance rather than a reality.

Compulsion does not feel like force. It feels like urgency. Attention narrows. The body tightens. Action feels required immediately. There is little space for reflection and little tolerance for delay. The internal pressure does not invite decision. It demands release. Afterward, relief arrives briefly. Then regret follows. Then the cycle resets.

One of the most confusing aspects of compulsion is how aggressively it is defended. When questioned, people react with irritation or hostility. When interrupted, they feel attacked. When confronted, they accuse others of control, fall silent, or deny that anything is happening at all. Speech collapses, thought withdraws, and a false reality is protected, not out of strategy, but out of shame.

This defensiveness is not about autonomy. It is about protection. Compulsion resists exposure.

As compulsion strengthens, the language around freedom begins to change. Freedom becomes the absence of restraint. Boundaries are framed as oppression. Discipline is framed as harm. The person no longer evaluates outcomes. They justify them.

Compulsion collapses time. Long-term consequences feel abstract. Immediate relief feels essential. The future loses weight, and the present dominates. People say they will deal with it later or that they no longer care. The seriousness is not debated. It is avoided.

Compulsion rarely operates without narrative. It recruits logic to defend itself. These justifications are not neutral thoughts. They are reinforcements that insulate behavior from challenge. Because compulsion uses the person's own desires, memories, and voice, it feels intimate.

The pattern repeats. Regret follows. Promises return and break again. What is presented as preference behaves like command.

As compulsion deepens, attempts to resist often provoke an emotional surge. Irritation turns to anger. Delay feels intolerable. Interruption feels hostile. This reaction is disproportionate to the situation. It is not disappointment. It is backlash.

When compulsion is mislabeled as freedom, accountability collapses. A person cannot challenge what they believe they have chosen. They cannot resist what they believe expresses them. This is why compulsion is so effective. It does not need secrecy. It only needs misidentification.

Choice preserves dignity. Compulsion erodes it. Choice strengthens agency. Compulsion consumes it. The difference is not moral. It is structural. One expands the self. The other replaces it.

What is rarely described is what happens at the exact moment a person tries to choose against the pattern. The decision does not feel dramatic. It feels small: a pause, a hesitation, a quiet recognition. Then something intervenes. The thought collapses before it can mature. The pause becomes agitation. The body moves before consent is given.

The person does not feel forced. They feel rushed. Afterwards, they are left confused, not about what they did, but about why the option not to do it never felt available. This is not temptation. Temptation allows refusal. This is compulsion that preempts choice.

Over time, people stop attempting resistance, not because they agree with the behavior, but because every attempt ends the same way—interrupted, overridden, unfinished. The will does not argue. It does not get the chance.

This chapter has not argued that every impulse is external. It has shown something simpler. When fragmentation divides the self, when numbness dulls resistance, when stillness is avoided, and when compulsion is defended as choice, the conditions for takeover are complete.

What comes next is not escalation. It is explanation.

Part III examines why modern frameworks—psychological, medical, and cultural—can describe these patterns with precision, yet remain unable to stop them. Description without authority leaves the door open.

There are people who still know who they are, and that is what makes this unbearable. They have not lost their values. They have not abandoned their conscience. They have not gone numb. They feel the misalignment every day.

They live in relationships that require them to shrink. They participate in conversations that ask them to betray their own clarity. They make choices that benefit a version of themselves they do not respect. And they know it.

This is the part no one talks about. This is not ignorance. It is compliance without consent.

They look at their lives and feel a quiet grief, not for what they lost, but for what they are actively living that does not represent them. They scroll past things they disagree with and feel their resistance soften, not because they changed their mind, but because they are tired of resisting.

They remain in systems that reward silence and punish conviction. They perform agreement because disagreement feels expensive. Later, alone, they replay the day. They remember the moment they should have spoken and did not. The decision that felt wrong and still happened. The boundary they felt dissolve again.

They do not excuse it. They do not justify it. They simply feel the weight of it. Somewhere inside, the real self is still awake, watching a life unfold that does not belong to them.

This is what occupation looks like when the mind is still conscious.

WHY MODERN EXPLANATIONS FAIL

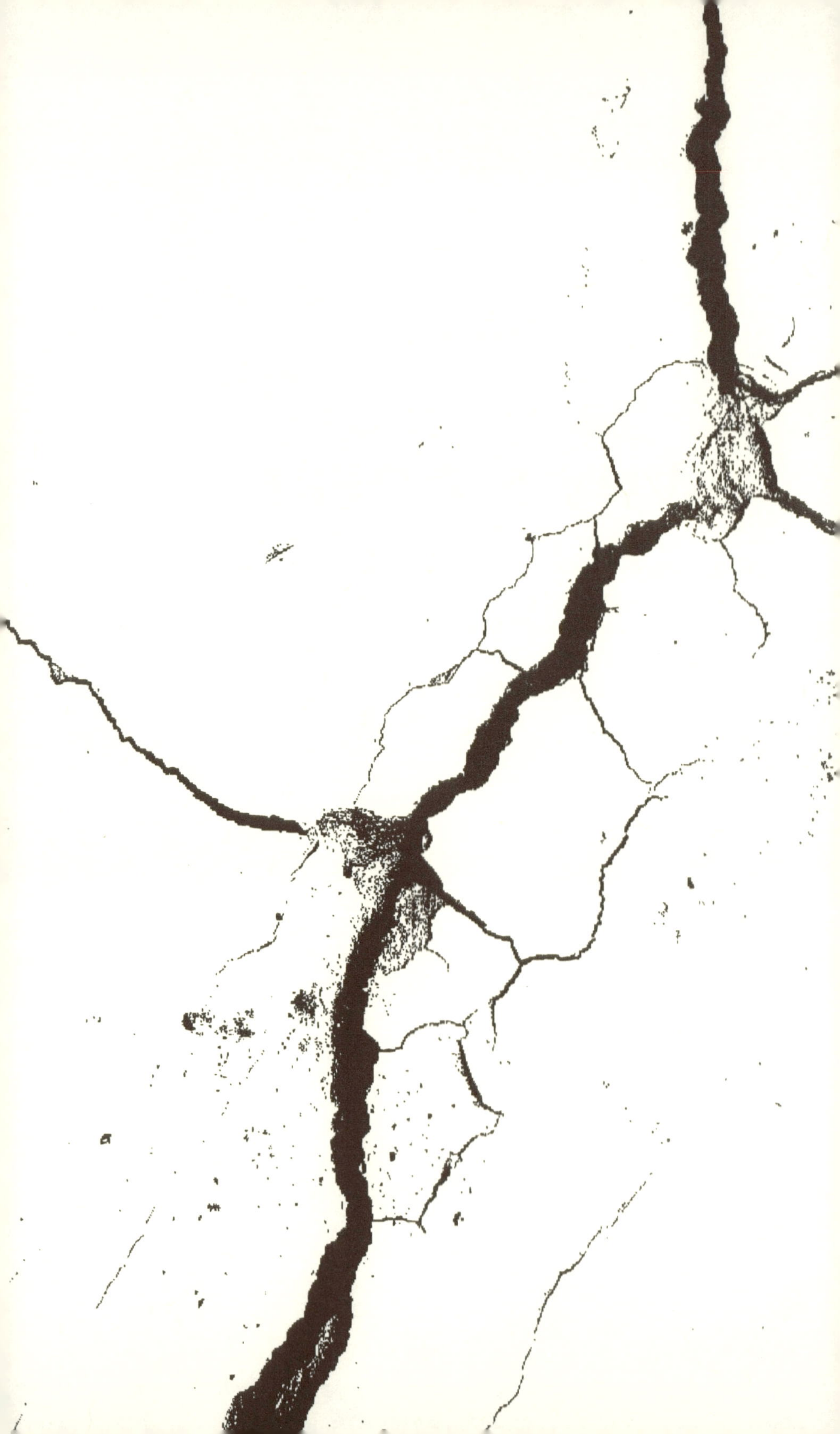

9

PSYCHOLOGY CAN DESCRIBE—BUT NOT REMOVE

Modern psychology is skilled at observation. It names patterns, tracks behavior, and maps cause and effect. For many people, this is profoundly helpful. Understanding one's history, wounds, and conditioning can bring relief, insight, and language to experiences that once felt chaotic.

But for a growing number of people, something unsettling happens after understanding arrives. Nothing changes.

Many individuals who feel internally displaced are not uninformed. They know their trauma. They recognize their triggers. They can articulate their attachment patterns, coping mechanisms, and defense strategies. Some can even predict their behavior with unsettling accuracy. And yet, when the moment comes to act differently, the same outcome repeats.

The problem is not ignorance. It is impotence.

Explanation answers the question why. Authority answers the question who decides. Psychology excels at the first. It was never designed to fully address the second. Understanding why an impulse exists does not automatically grant the power to refuse it. Knowing the origin of a thought does not ensure the ability to dismiss it. Insight can illuminate the mechanism without restoring command.

This is not a failure of psychology. It is a limitation of scope.

Many therapeutic models assume that once something is made conscious, it loses power. Sometimes this is true. But many people discover the opposite. The more clearly they see the pattern, the more entrenched it becomes. They understand it, label it, and discuss it. And still, it overrides them. At that point, awareness becomes a witness rather than a governor.

For some, therapy becomes cyclical. Each session produces insight. Each insight produces temporary relief. Each relief fades. The person returns with the same struggle—now better articulated, but no less dominant. They are not regressing. They are stalled. An unspoken conclusion begins to form: if understanding does not restore agency, what does?

Many modern frameworks describe the mind as a collection of parts, each with its own needs, fears, and motivations. This language can be compassionate and useful. But it encounters a serious problem when a "part" refuses integration. Some inner forces do not soften when acknowledged. They do not negotiate. They do not stand down when understood. They resist hierarchy. And without hierarchy, there is no authority—only endless conversation.

Compassion is necessary. But compassion without command creates vulnerability. When every impulse is treated as wounded and worthy of accommodation, the self loses the right to say no. Boundaries dissolve under the weight of understanding. The result is not healing. It is paralysis.

When psychological tools fail to restore control, the failure is often internalized. The person assumes they did not do the work correctly. They believe they have not healed deeply enough. They conclude they are resisting unconsciously, or that they are too damaged to recover. This compounds the problem. The self is blamed for its own displacement.

Psychology can describe behavior without assigning moral direction. It can explain impulse without calling it wrong. It can map desire without judging its aim. It can analyze conflict without naming allegiance. This neutrality is intentional and valuable. But it leaves one critical question unanswered: what happens when something within the mind does not seek healing, balance, or integration at all?

Psychology can interpret. It cannot command. It can advise. It cannot evict. It can illuminate patterns. It cannot exercise authority over them. When the problem is not confusion but takeover, description alone is insufficient.

This chapter does not argue against psychology. It establishes a boundary. There are moments when explanation reaches its limit, when the issue is no longer understanding but governance. When the self knows what is happening, knows why it is happening, and still cannot intervene, something else is required.

Not something that negotiates. Something that commands.

The next chapter examines medication—another powerful intervention—and why symptom relief, while often necessary, does not resolve the deeper question of control. Because when authority is missing, relief is not the same as freedom.

10

MEDICATION WITHOUT MASTERY

Medication can be life-saving. For many people, it stabilizes mood, reduces intensity, and creates enough space to function. It can quiet symptoms that would otherwise overwhelm daily life and prevent collapse. None of this is denied here.

But for those who feel internally displaced, medication often produces a troubling realization. The symptoms are quieter. The struggle remains.

Medication is designed to reduce intensity. It dampens anxiety, lifts depression, slows compulsive loops, and blunts emotional extremes. For many, this brings immediate relief. But relief does not equal mastery. A person may feel calmer yet still overridden, more functional yet not more sovereign, less distressed yet no more in control. The problem has been softened, not resolved.

One of the most consistent observations among those medicated for long periods is this: the will does not strengthen. A person may feel less pain, but not more authority. They may feel more stable, but not more able to choose against impulse. The internal hierarchy remains compromised. Medication adjusts chemistry. It does not restore command.

In some cases, medication makes displacement harder to detect. Behavior improves. Crises diminish. Outward stability returns. But inwardly, the person may still feel absent from themselves. They are quieter, but not freer. Less reactive, but not more present. Everything looks better. Nothing feels resolved.

Long-term medication often involves an unspoken trade: reduced suffering in exchange for reduced sensitivity. Emotional range narrows. Urgency dulls. Desire flattens. For some, this trade is necessary. For others, it deepens the sense of disconnection. They are less distressed, but also less alive.

When agency does not return, the solution is often assumed to be chemical. The dose is increased. Medications are switched. Another prescription is added. Sometimes this helps. But many discover that no combination restores what is missing. The problem was never purely biochemical. Chemical changes alter the environment. They do not reclaim authority.

Medication is often framed as management. You will always have this. This keeps it under control. This helps you cope. Management assumes permanence. It prepares the person to coexist with the problem rather than confront it. For those experiencing internal takeover, this framing quietly reinforces resignation.

This chapter is not a call to reject medication. For some, it is necessary. For others, it is stabilizing. For many, it prevents harm. The issue is not use. It is expectation. Medication can support healing. It cannot replace authority. Removing it does not restore command. Keeping it does not create it.

What is rarely discussed is the absence of mastery. People are taught how to manage symptoms, but not how to reclaim internal leadership. They are guided toward coping, but not command. A quiet question forms: if chemistry is stabilized, insight is gained, and behavior is managed, why does the self still feel displaced?

Across psychology and medication, a pattern emerges. Symptoms can be reduced. Awareness can be increased. Behavior can be managed. Yet authority remains absent. This suggests the problem is not simply emotional, cognitive, or chemical. Something else is missing.

This absence does not remain confined to the inner world. It begins to shape how people relate.

Most people do not leave relationships when something goes wrong. They stay. Staying is not always loyalty. Sometimes it is erosion. They stop bringing things up, not because the issues resolved, but because raising them feels exhausting. They sense when honesty will create tension and quietly choose comfort instead.

They learn which topics tighten the room and which ones keep it calm. They adjust. Over time, conversation becomes selective. They speak about logistics, schedules, and surface matters that do not risk disruption. What they do not say accumulates. Disappointments go unnamed. Boundaries soften. Expectations lower, not consciously, but gradually.

They tell themselves they are being patient, understanding, mature. But something else is happening. Each unspoken truth creates distance. Each avoided conversation trains the self to stay quiet. Each compromise that is not mutual takes something with it. Intimacy fades not because of conflict, but because of accommodation.

They begin to feel lonely inside the relationship—present but not fully known, engaged but not fully expressed. Because there is no explosion, no betrayal, and no obvious wrongdoing, it is difficult to name what is wrong. From the outside, the relationship looks stable. Inside, the person feels thinner.

They miss themselves as they were before they learned to disappear to keep the peace.

This is one of the clearest external signs of occupation. Not abandonment by others, but self-abandonment in proximity. The body stays. The role remains. The self retreats. And because nothing visibly breaks, nothing demands repair. The relationship continues, and the cost becomes invisible, even to the one paying it.

This chapter does not dismiss medical intervention. It exposes its limit. When relief does not restore agency and management does not restore command, the explanation must expand.

The next chapter examines trauma, one of the most widely accepted explanations for fragmentation, and why even deep healing of the past sometimes fails to restore the self. Because when agency is missing, the cause may not be behind you. It may be operating in the present.

11

TRAUMA IS NOT THE WHOLE STORY

Trauma matters. It shapes perception, behavior, and belief. It alters the nervous system, fragments memory, and teaches the mind to anticipate threat even when none is present. Ignoring trauma leads to shallow explanations and ineffective solutions. But elevating trauma to a universal explanation creates a different problem.

For many people, trauma has been thoroughly addressed, and the sense of internal displacement remains.

Many individuals who feel overridden have done extensive trauma work. They can name what happened and understand how it affected them. They have processed memories, reframed narratives, and rebuilt context. Some have forgiven. Some have grieved. Some have healed relationships long thought impossible. And yet, the core struggle persists.

They are not reliving the past. They are being overruled in the present.

Trauma explains why certain sensitivities exist. It explains hypervigilance, avoidance, emotional reactivity, and distrust. It explains how the nervous system learned to protect itself under threat. What it does not automatically explain is the loss of command.

A person can understand their trauma and still feel unable to resist impulses that violate their values. They can heal memories and still feel divided in action. They can feel compassion for their younger self and still feel hijacked by something that does not resemble fear at all. At that point, trauma no longer fits the entire picture.

One of the most telling clues that trauma is not the sole cause is timing. Trauma occurred in the past, but many people describe the intensification of their struggle as recent, sometimes sudden, sometimes years after stability was established. They may say they were functioning well for years, that it started long after therapy, and that they believed they had already dealt with all of it.

The disruption does not follow the expected timeline. This suggests the influence is not only historical.

Trauma work often brings relief. Triggers soften. Reactions slow. Perspective widens. But for some, one thing does not return: authority.

They feel calmer but not stronger. More aware but not more capable of resistance. Less reactive but no more decisive. Healing the wound does not always reclaim the will.

As trauma frameworks have become more central, they have also become more expansive. Trauma has quietly turned into a catch-all explanation. Any discomfort is traced backward. Any resistance is interpreted as fear. Any moral struggle is reframed as injury.

This framework offers compassion, but it also removes responsibility and obscures agency. When every impulse is attributed to pain, the question of command disappears.

For some, trauma work becomes perpetual. Each layer reveals another. Each memory points to a deeper one. Each insight suggests more processing is needed. Healing becomes a moving target. Meanwhile, the present remains ungoverned. The person understands themselves deeply but cannot direct themselves effectively.

One of the clearest distinctions between trauma response and takeover is direction. Trauma responses aim toward safety. They avoid pain and seek protection. But many people experience impulses that actively undermine safety, stability, and coherence, even when no threat is present. They are drawn toward destruction, not protection.

This is not fear-based behavior. It is something else.

When everything is misdiagnosed as trauma, displacement can deepen rather than resolve. The person is told they are not responsible, that this is not really them, that they are reacting. But if the behavior continues and worsens, this framing becomes confusing rather than healing. The person is left with awareness but no authority.

This chapter does not diminish trauma. It places it accurately. Trauma can fracture the self, weaken boundaries, and open doors. But it does not explain everything that walks through.

When the past has been addressed, the nervous system stabilized, and understanding achieved, yet agency remains absent, another question emerges. What is operating now? Not what happened then. Not what was learned before. But what is influencing the present moment.

Psychology explains patterns. Medication manages symptoms. Trauma work heals wounds. And yet, for some, the self remains displaced.

The next chapter confronts what modern frameworks refuse to name—the category they avoid not because it lacks evidence, but because it challenges their assumptions. Because when every explanation fails, silence is not neutrality. It is omission.

12

THE MISSING CATEGORY

When every available explanation has been applied and something essential remains unresolved, the problem is not complexity. It is absence.

Modern frameworks explain much. They describe patterns of behavior, map neural pathways, and contextualize emotional responses. They offer language where there was once confusion. But they also share a common boundary. There are questions they do not ask.

Psychology, psychiatry, and contemporary cultural models differ in approach, but they converge on one assumption: all internal experience originates from the self. Thoughts may be distorted. Impulses may be conditioned. Desires may be maladaptive. But they are assumed to be owned.

This assumption is rarely examined because it is foundational. Questioning it destabilizes the entire framework, so it is not questioned.

A closed system can describe endlessly, but it cannot account for intrusion. If all influence is assumed to be internal, then any experience of override must be reframed as pathology, resistance, or immaturity. There is no other category available. The system does not ask what this force is. It asks why the person is failing to manage it. The burden always returns to the self.

Because the missing category cannot be named, experiences that point toward it are softened or rewritten. Being overridden becomes dysregulation. Internal hostility becomes negative self-talk. Compulsion becomes coping. Moral conflict becomes shame. These translations are not malicious. They are protective. They keep the system intact.

And yet the pattern refuses to disappear.

Across individuals, cultures, and histories, the same experiences recur: thoughts that feel foreign, a will that no longer responds, an aversion to truth, stillness, and integration, and a pull toward destruction that contradicts self-interest. These experiences are ancient. They are not new, and they are not culture-bound. What is new is the refusal to classify them honestly.

To acknowledge intrusion is to admit that the self is not always sovereign, that there may be influence without consent, direction without agreement, and pressure without origin in trauma, chemistry, or memory. This challenges the modern emphasis on autonomy and control. So the possibility is excluded, not disproven.

When a category is missing, misdiagnosis becomes inevitable. People are told to heal wounds that are not causing the behavior, to manage symptoms that are not the source of control, and to negotiate with forces that do not negotiate. When these approaches fail, the conclusion is predictable. The person is blamed.

Despite the system's refusal, the language slips out anyway. People say it feels like something took over, that they do not feel like themselves, that they are not in control anymore, that there is something in them they cannot stop. These phrases persist because they describe reality more accurately than the alternatives. They point toward a category that has not disappeared, only been renamed out of existence.

This chapter does not claim that every struggle is external. It does not deny biology, trauma, or psychology. It identifies something simpler: influence does not always originate from the self. When that possibility is excluded, solutions remain incomplete.

If intrusion exists, even rarely, entire approaches must change. Authority becomes central. Boundaries become essential. Resistance becomes meaningful again. Without this category, the self is left defenseless, armed only with insight and management.

So far, this book has traced a pattern—from loss of agency, to fragmentation, to numbness, to compulsion, to explanations that describe but do not restore. What remains unspoken, but increasingly unavoidable, is this: if something is operating that does not seek healing, integration, or freedom, then it must be confronted, not managed.

The next chapter steps across that threshold. It examines possession without spectacle, not as myth or horror, but as a quiet, modern process that thrives precisely because it goes unnamed. What cannot be named cannot be resisted.

Most people do not think of themselves as changed. They think of themselves as tired, stressed, or pressed by circumstances. When they notice their behavior shifting, they explain it away. They snap more easily, withdraw faster, and care less about things that once mattered. They tell themselves it is temporary.

But the changes persist. They hear themselves speak with a sharpness that does not feel natural. They react with indifference where concern once lived. They choose convenience over integrity without noticing the trade. Later, sometimes much later, there is a moment of recognition. That was not me.

Not because the action was dramatic or extreme, but because it did not match their internal sense of who they are. They do not feel evil. They feel unfamiliar.

Friends notice before they do. Someone says they have changed. Someone hesitates before opening up. Someone stops expecting warmth. Instead of examining this, people defend themselves. They say they are being realistic, stronger, less naïve. But underneath the explanation is discomfort.

Strength does not usually feel like shrinking. Realism does not usually feel like betrayal. What is happening is not moral collapse. It is displacement.

The person is still there, but no longer steering. Reactions replace responses. Habits replace values. Efficiency replaces care. Because the world rewards this sharper, quieter, more compliant version, the change accelerates. People adapt to who they have become because it works. It gets results, reduces friction, and keeps things moving.

But it costs something subtle and profound. They lose trust in themselves, not consciously, but quietly. They stop relying on their own instincts. They stop recognizing their reflection in their behavior. They stop feeling anchored to a consistent inner identity.

And when someone finally asks, "Is this really who you are now?" they do not know how to answer.

PART 4

POSSESSION WITHOUT SPECTACLE

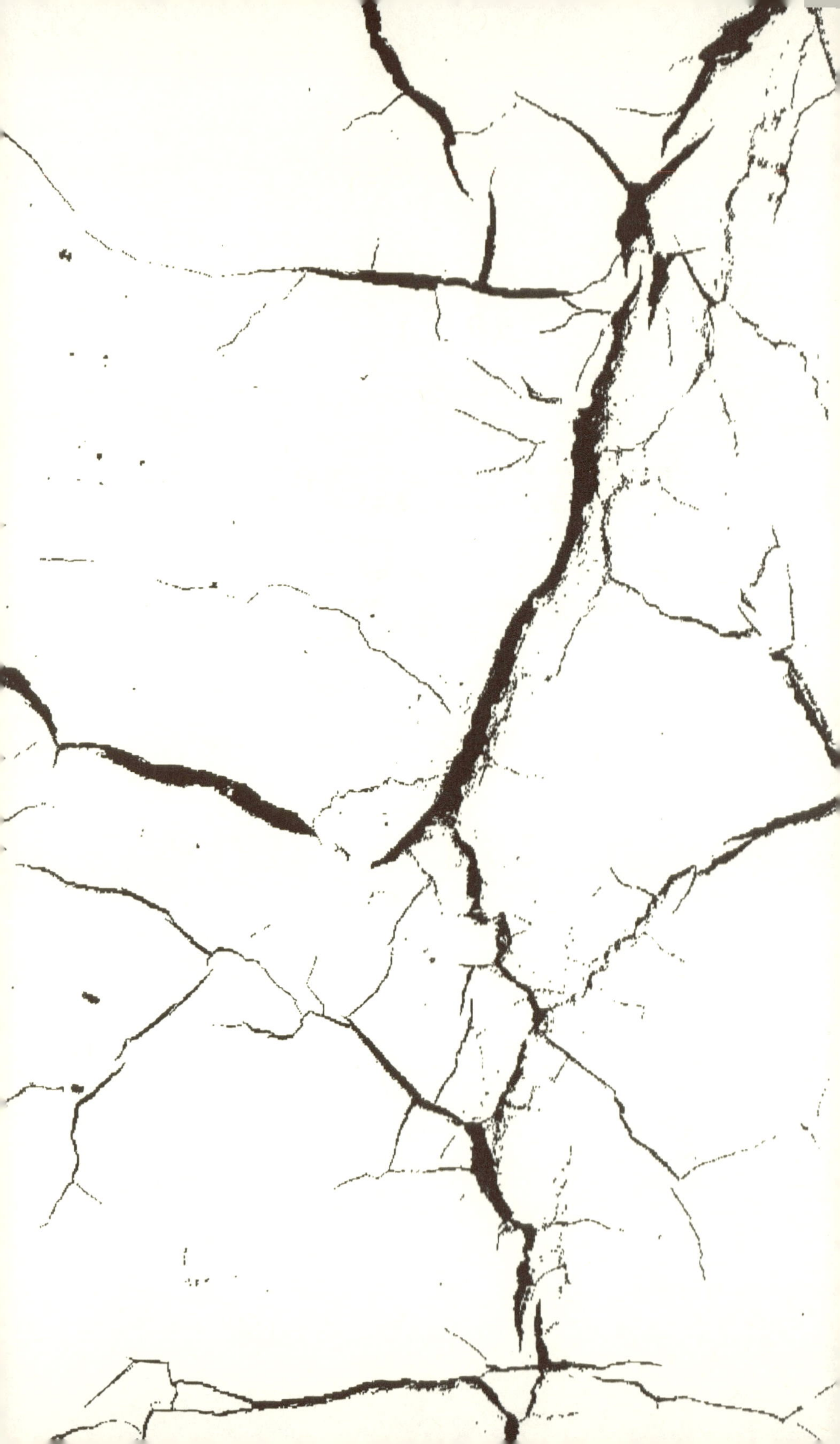

13

POSSESSION ISN'T DRAMATIC ANYMORE

When most people hear the word possession, they picture spectacle. Violence, strange voices, loss of physical control, and scenes designed to provoke fear. Because of that imagery, the concept is often dismissed entirely.

But what if the problem is not exaggeration, but misrepresentation?

If possession exists in the modern world, it would not resemble its older portrayals. It would adapt. It would avoid attention and disruption. It would avoid anything that invites intervention. It would not announce itself. It would blend.

Overt possession invites resistance. Quiet possession prevents it. A person who screams for help draws attention. A person who feels subtly "off" yet remains functional does not.

Modern possession does not remove a person from society. It keeps them participating—working, consuming, reacting, and repeating. They appear externally normal while remaining internally displaced. Spectacle is unnecessary when influence operates internally.

There is no need to control the body when the will can be bypassed. No need to silence speech when thought can be redirected. No need to dominate when the person can be convinced they are choosing. The most efficient form of control is consent that is not real.

This modern form does not replace the self entirely. It crowds it out. The person remains present but no longer decisive. Conscience still speaks but no longer governs. Judgment exists but no longer directs. This is not annihilation. It is occupation.

A possessed person, in the modern sense, does not look dangerous. They look distracted, fragmented, compelled, and defensive. They insist nothing is wrong. They resist stillness. They react strongly to truth. They feel hostility toward integration. And they believe these reactions are their own.

One of the most reliable indicators of possession is not immorality. It is aversion to order. Order requires hierarchy. Hierarchy requires authority. Authority threatens displacement.

This is why clarity feels abrasive, discipline feels oppressive, and truth feels aggressive. Not because these things harm the person, but because they restore command.

A tired mind does not resist well. Chronic stimulation, emotional overload, and constant urgency are not accidental side effects of modern life. They are ideal conditions. Exhaustion weakens boundaries. Overwhelm collapses hierarchy. Busyness prevents reflection. A rested, unified person is harder to occupy.

The greatest advantage of modern possession is plausibility. Every symptom has an explanation. Every behavior has a diagnosis. Every impulse has a justification. Nothing needs to be named. And what is never named is never confronted.

When possession operates quietly, it merges with identity. The person does not feel invaded. They feel expressed. So when something challenges the influence, it feels personal. Correction feels like attack. Resistance feels like oppression. Authority feels dangerous. The defense is instinctive.

Management assumes cooperation. Possession does not cooperate. It adapts, hides, and waits. Reducing symptoms does not remove influence. Understanding patterns does not restore command. Avoidance does not reclaim authority. Only confrontation does.

This chapter does not claim that every struggle is possession. It makes a narrower and more dangerous claim: possession no longer needs to be extreme to be effective. It only needs to be subtle.

Possession is not about losing consciousness. It is about losing command. When the self can no longer govern thought, desire, restraint, and action, something else already is.

From this point forward, the book no longer circles the possibility. It names it, not to provoke fear, but to restore defense. Because what is named can be resisted.

The next chapter examines the inner voice that actively resists healing, wholeness, and responsibility, and why that resistance is not accidental.

14

THE VOICE THAT HATES YOU BECOMING WHOLE

ost people assume that if something exists inside them, it must want what is best for them. This assumption feels reasonable. After all, why would any part of the inner world oppose healing, clarity, or peace?

But many people discover, quietly and reluctantly, that something within them does exactly that.

A strange pattern often emerges when a person begins to regain clarity. They make progress. They feel steadier. They sense alignment returning. And then, without warning, resistance appears. Not discouragement or fatigue, but opposition.

Thoughts surface that undermine momentum. Emotions intensify without cause. Behaviors sabotage progress in ways that feel deliberate rather than accidental. The reaction is disproportionate. Healing should feel relieving. Instead, it feels contested.

This resistance has a distinct voice. It is not confused or curious, and it is not seeking understanding. It does not say that it is afraid or that it needs time. It says the effort will fail anyway, that trying is pointless, that the person is pretending, that they should just stop. Its aim is not caution. It is termination.

This is one of the ways it differs from fear. Fear wants safety. Fear seeks avoidance. Fear retreats when reassurance is offered. This voice does not. It persists even when safety is established. It intensifies when clarity increases. It grows louder when progress is made. Fear resists pain. This voice resists wholeness.

People often describe moments where they knowingly undermine themselves. They break commitments without necessity. They abandon practices that were helping. They provoke conflict that damages connection. Later, they ask why they did that. The answer is not confusion. They knew better. They did it anyway.

The resistance carries a particular emotional signature. It is sharp, contemptuous, and impatient. It does not negotiate. It does not soften. It wants collapse, not compromise.

Self-compassion is essential for healing, but it has limits. When directed toward fear or pain, compassion calms and integrates. When directed toward this resistance, compassion is ignored or exploited. The voice does not want comfort. It wants authority removed.

Modern frameworks often assume the inner world is cooperative at its core, that all internal parts ultimately seek balance, safety, or healing. This assumption fails when confronted with resistance that actively opposes restoration. Not everything inside the mind wants harmony. Some forces benefit from fragmentation.

One of the clearest indicators of this voice is its reaction to responsibility. Responsibility feels oppressive. Accountability feels hostile. Commitment feels threatening, not because these things are difficult, but because they restore command. Wholeness requires authorship, and this voice resists authorship at all costs.

As healing progresses, the self becomes more integrated. Boundaries return. Values regain weight. The will strengthens. This reduces access, and reduced access provokes retaliation. Sabotage increases precisely because the window is closing.

This chapter does not claim that every negative thought is external. It identifies something specific: a pattern of resistance that intensifies with healing, opposes clarity, undermines responsibility, and seeks fragmentation. This is not self-doubt. It is hostility toward wholeness.

As long as this voice is mistaken for the self, it holds authority. The person defers to it, obeys it, and defends it. Once it is recognized as opposition rather than identity, its power weakens. What is seen can be resisted.

Anything that hates your becoming whole does not have your best interest at heart. That is not metaphor. It is discernment.

This chapter has identified opposition. The next chapter examines how this opposition expresses itself behaviorally, through repeated self-sabotage that feels foreign, compulsive, and destructive. When resistance turns active, it begins to act.

Moral confusion rarely arrives as rebellion. It arrives as justification. People do not wake up one day believing the opposite of what they once believed. They wake up believing it is complicated.

They start making exceptions, not because their values changed, but because their circumstances did. They excuse behavior they would have condemned in someone else. They overlook actions that benefit them while criticizing the same actions when they do not. They defend positions they privately feel uneasy about.

The discomfort does not come from not knowing what is right. It comes from knowing and navigating around it. They still feel a twinge when something crosses a line, but instead of stopping, they explain.

They cite nuance, context, and intentions. They say it is not that simple, that others need to understand the situation, that there are reasons. Sometimes there are. But what has changed is not their ability to reason. It is their willingness to let reason override conscience.

They begin to argue both sides of an issue depending on what is convenient. They shift standards quietly. They apply principles selectively, not out of malice, but out of self-preservation. Holding consistent convictions would require change, and change would threaten the life they are already maintaining.

Clarity becomes inconvenient. Language softens. Definitions blur. Firm positions are avoided. They do not feel dishonest. They feel flexible. But flexibility without an anchor does not lead to wisdom. It leads to drift.

Over time, they lose confidence in their own moral compass. They hesitate before calling something wrong. They feel embarrassed naming what feels obvious. They become suspicious of certainty, especially in others.

When someone speaks with clarity, it feels abrasive, judgmental, or unsafe, not because clarity is cruel, but because it exposes confusion they have learned to live inside.

This is how moral confusion stabilizes, not by erasing values, but by surrounding them with enough caveats that they no longer guide behavior. People do not stop believing in right and wrong. They stop trusting themselves to name it.

At a certain point, people stop evaluating reality for themselves, not because they become careless, but because discernment becomes exhausting. They look outward instead of inward. They listen for cues. They measure reactions.

They begin asking not whether something is true, but whether it is acceptable. Consensus becomes the guide. If everyone agrees, resistance feels unnecessary. If everyone repeats it, doubt feels foolish. If everyone participates, objection feels dangerous.

Discernment requires internal authority. Consensus removes the need for it. People adopt positions they have not examined, repeat language they would not have chosen, and defend ideas they privately feel uneasy about, not because they are convinced, but because alignment reduces friction.

Over time, consensus begins to feel like safety. Standing alone feels reckless. Questioning feels arrogant. Clarity feels disruptive. So people outsource judgment. They borrow certainty instead of forming it. They defer rather than decide. They mirror instead of discern.

Because everyone around them is doing the same thing, the loss goes unnoticed. No one feels controlled. They feel aligned.

This is how mass compliance forms without coercion, not through force, but through exhaustion. Discernment fades not because it is wrong, but because it requires a self that still holds authority. When that authority is gone, consensus becomes the substitute.

And the substitute feels convincing.

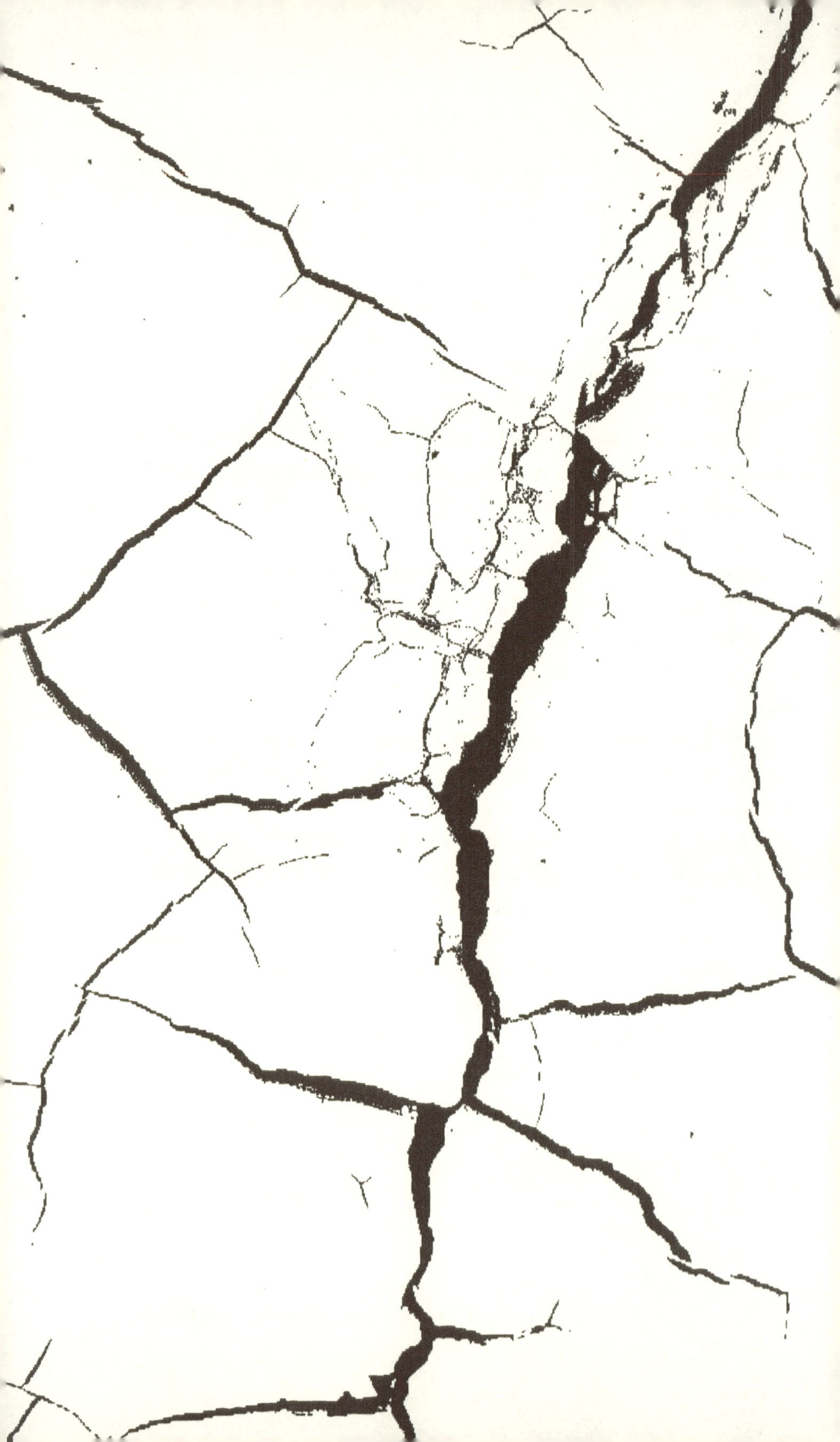

15

SELF-SABOTAGE AS AN EXTERNAL WILL

Most people believe self-sabotage is irrational. They assume it comes from fear, insecurity, or unresolved pain. They are told they are protecting themselves from disappointment, failure, or vulnerability. Sometimes that is true.

But there is a form of self-sabotage that does not protect. It destroys.

This form becomes visible when harm is chosen without benefit. There is no comfort afterward, no safety gained, and no anxiety reduced. The person does not feel protected. They feel diminished. They look back and think that it cost them everything, that they knew better, that they do not understand why they did that.

This is not avoidance. It is violation.

What makes this form of sabotage distinct is its precision. It does not attack randomly. It targets moments of stability, emerging clarity, meaningful relationships, and long-term progress. The timing is exact. Just as momentum builds, something intervenes. Just as coherence returns, something disrupts it.

This is not clumsiness. It is strategy.

People often describe this experience as being on autopilot. They are present but not directing. They watch themselves send the message they should not send, make the choice they already decided against, and abandon the commitment that mattered most. There is a brief internal protest. Then silence. The action proceeds anyway.

This is not impulsivity. Impulsivity is fast. This is deliberate. The person may hesitate, argue internally, or even pause. Then they proceed, knowing the outcome. Impulsivity bypasses awareness. This bypasses authority.

One of the most disturbing aspects of this sabotage is what follows. Clarity returns immediately. The person sees the damage clearly, feels the loss acutely, and understands exactly what happened. There is no confusion. Only grief and a sense of being overridden.

This rules out ignorance.

Guilt, in these cases, does not correct the pattern. Guilt is meant to restore alignment. Here, remorse does not prevent repetition. The person feels regret deeply and yet repeats the behavior. This produces despair. They wonder what will stop them if guilt does not.

The answer is not more guilt.

This form of self-sabotage often arrives with pressure. There is a narrowing sensation, a tightening urgency, and a sense that something must be done immediately. Delay feels unbearable. Reflection feels impossible. This pressure is not emotional overflow. It is directive.

People frequently say that it did not feel like them, that they do not know where it came from, that it was like something took over. These are not excuses. They are accurate descriptions.

The behavior does not align with the person's values, goals, or identity. It aligns with interference.

This distinction matters. The will is not destroyed. The conscience still speaks. Judgment still functions. They are simply ignored. Something else issues the final instruction.

This pattern persists because it is effective. It restores fragmentation, reopens access, and dissolves progress. After sabotage, the person feels demoralized, ashamed, and less likely to attempt change again. This creates compliance.

Modern language often reframes sabotage as self-expression. People are told they are not ready, that they are honoring their truth, that they are listening to themselves. But honoring destruction does not lead to freedom. It leads to erosion.

The self makes mistakes. An external will makes patterns. When the same form of destruction repeats despite insight, remorse, and effort, authorship must be questioned.

This chapter does not claim that every failure is external. It identifies something specific. When sabotage targets wholeness, arrives with pressure, bypasses authority, and leaves clarity intact, it is not merely internal struggle. It is opposition enacted.

So far, the pattern is clear. Authority erodes. Resistance is opposed. Sabotage restores access.

The next chapter examines this pattern across lives, cultures, and histories, not to sensationalize it, but to show its consistency. Because when the same strategy appears everywhere, it is no longer personal.

16

THE PATTERN NO ONE WANTS TO NAME

By this point, the experience no longer feels isolated. What began as a personal struggle now reveals a shape—a sequence that repeats across individuals who have never met, in cultures that never coordinated, across eras with no shared language. Different lives and different personalities follow the same progression. This is not coincidence.

Again and again, the same pattern emerges. There is a gradual loss of inner authority. Thoughts begin to feel hostile or imposed. Aversion to stillness, clarity, and order intensifies. Compulsion is framed as freedom. Sabotage restores fragmentation just as coherence begins to return. The details vary. The structure does not.

Cultural influence shapes values and behavior, but it does not produce the same internal experience across vastly different contexts. Yet people separated by geography, class, belief, and background describe the same sensations: being overridden, being driven, being divided, and being opposed when they try to heal. This points to something more fundamental than social conditioning. Culture may provide the cover. It does not generate the pattern.

Long before modern psychology, people recognized this phenomenon intuitively. They lacked clinical terminology, but not perception. They spoke of inner division, loss of command, hostile thoughts, and destructive urges that did not align with identity. What differs today is not the experience. It is the refusal to name it.

Because the language has been removed, individuals assume their experience is unique or shameful. They think no one else would understand this, that something must be wrong with them, that they cannot say this out loud. Isolation deepens the problem. What remains unspoken cannot be confronted.

The pattern survives because every part of it can be explained away. Thoughts are labeled symptoms. Compulsions are reframed as coping. Sabotage is explained as fear. Resistance is attributed to trauma. Each label contains truth, but none contain authority. Together, they obscure the whole.

This phenomenon is not limited to the visibly broken or struggling. It appears in people who are educated, disciplined, financially secure, and socially respected. External success does not prevent internal displacement. In some cases, it accelerates it. When identity is built outwardly, the inner world is left unattended.

The most revealing feature of this pattern is not dysfunction. It is resistance to integration. Anything that would restore coherence—stillness, responsibility, moral clarity, wholeness—provokes opposition. Not discomfort. Opposition. This reaction is not accidental.

To name the pattern is to admit that something other than the self may be operating. That admission threatens modern assumptions about autonomy and control. So the pattern is softened, reframed, or ignored—not because it lacks evidence, but because it demands response.

When a pattern goes unnamed, it goes unchallenged. People continue managing symptoms instead of confronting influence. They exhaust themselves trying to heal something that does not want healing. Eventually, many stop trying altogether. This is not peace. It is surrender.

Left unaddressed, this progression does not stabilize. It deepens. Authority continues to erode. Resistance weakens. Compulsion strengthens. Identity thins. What began as influence moves toward occupation.

This chapter does not ask the reader to accept a conclusion. It asks them to acknowledge a pattern. Recognition is the first act of resistance. Until something is seen clearly, it cannot be opposed.

Up to this point, the book has been descriptive. From here forward, it becomes prescriptive—not in tactics, but in posture. The next section examines false forms of resistance, paths that promise escape but ultimately strengthen the very forces they claim to oppose. Not every attempt at freedom leads away from control. Some lead deeper into it.

Most relationships do not fracture through confrontation. They thin. There is no fight to point to, no defining argument, no moment that explains the shift. There is only space.

People talk less, not because there is nothing to say, but because saying it feels heavy. They share selectively. They edit themselves without realizing they are doing it. The relationship becomes efficient. Necessary information is exchanged. Plans are coordinated. Responsibilities are managed. What disappears is curiosity.

They stop asking real questions. They stop pressing gently into each other's inner worlds. They stop noticing what has changed, not out of indifference, but out of fatigue. Distance feels safer than friction.

They tell themselves it is normal, that this is what long-term relationships look like, that closeness fades and stability replaces it. But stability without connection is just coexistence.

They feel it most in small moments. Silence stretches longer than it used to. Eye contact breaks sooner. Laughter does not linger. They sit near each other without actually meeting.

Because there is no obvious problem, there is nothing to fix. No one is angry. No one is leaving. No one is clearly at fault. So the distance goes unnamed.

Over time, people stop expecting to be fully known. They bring less of themselves into the room. They share fewer unfiltered thoughts. They keep more things private, not because they are hiding, but because it does not feel worth explaining. The relationship remains intact, but something essential is missing.

The most unsettling part is this: if someone were to ask what changed, they would not know how to answer. Nothing happened. That is the point.

This is relational distance, not created by conflict, but by quiet retreat. A gradual stepping back that feels reasonable in the moment and irreversible later. Because it does not hurt sharply, it is easy to live with—until one day, people realize they are closer to strangers than to the person sitting beside them.

PART 5

RESISTANCE AND FALSE ESCAPES

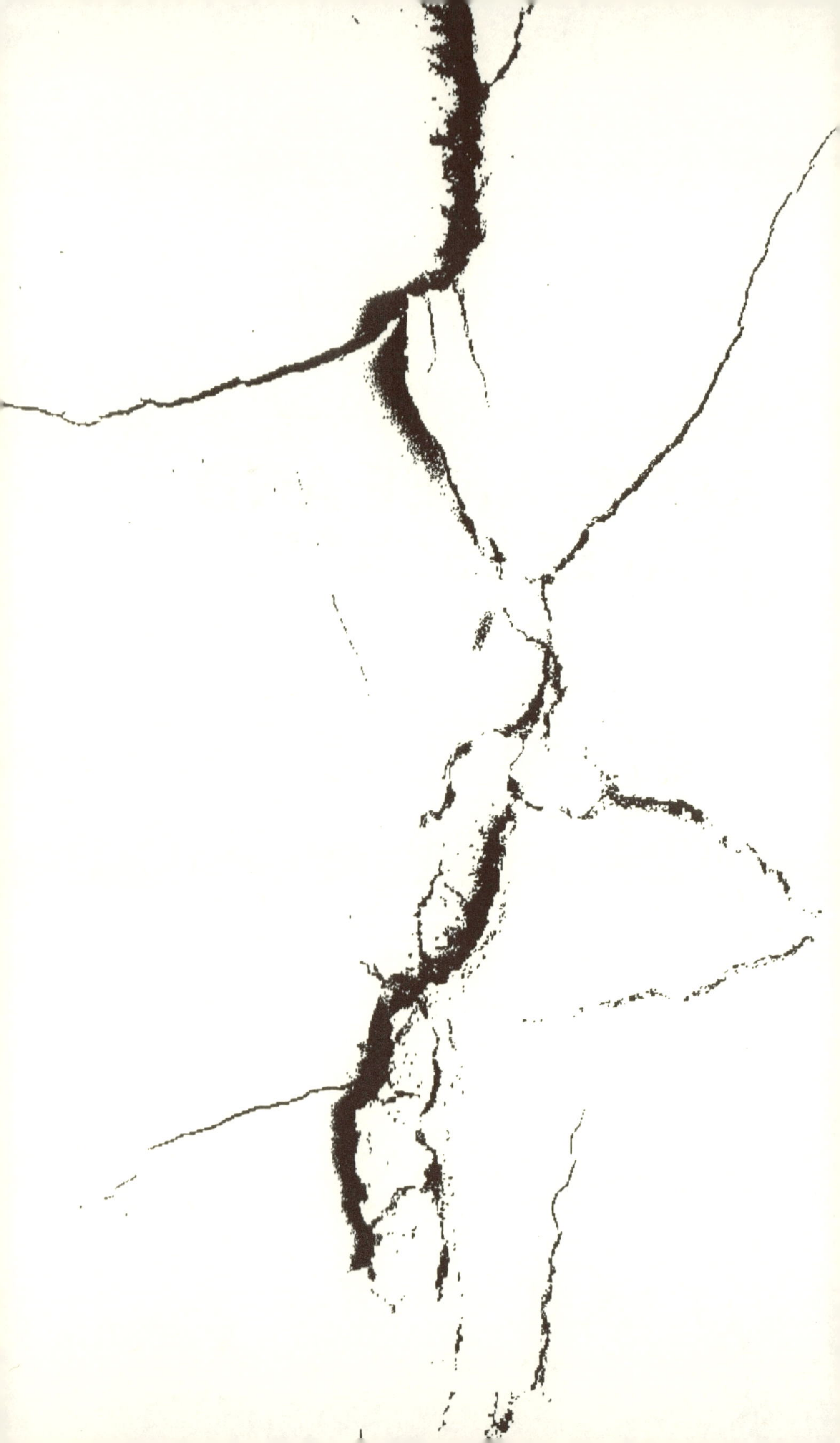

17

SELF-HELP AS SUBSTITUTION

When people sense they are losing control of their inner world, they do not remain passive. They search. They read. They listen. They attempt to improve themselves. This instinct is not misguided. It reflects a remaining desire for agency and wholeness. But for many people, the outcome is unsettling: the more they focus on fixing themselves, the less authority they seem to have.

Modern self-help is built on a compelling promise. If a person understands themselves deeply enough, disciplines their behavior consistently enough, and applies the right strategies faithfully enough, control can be restored. In many areas of life, this is true. Skill can be learned. Habits can be changed. Insight can improve outcomes. But for people experiencing internal displacement, self-help produces a different result. It increases effort without restoring command.

At first, self-help feels productive. It offers structure, language, and momentum. It provides explanations that make the experience intelligible and techniques that create temporary improvement. But over time, something subtle occurs. The focus shifts from authority to optimization. The question is no longer who is in charge, but what method should I try next. Control becomes procedural rather than positional.

Many people become trapped in cycles of improvement. A new book brings clarity. A new framework produces hope. A new routine generates momentum. Then the effect fades. Another method is sought. The person is not failing. They are substituting. Technique replaces authority. Insight replaces command. Effort replaces governance.

Self-help is especially appealing to the displaced because it keeps control internal. It reassures the person that the solution is already within them. They are told they have what they need; they simply have not accessed it correctly yet. For someone who already senses they are no longer in charge, this message sounds empowering. In practice, it becomes exhausting.

Over time, self-help often intensifies shame. When progress collapses, the conclusion is rarely that the framework is insufficient. Instead, the person assumes personal failure. They believe they lacked discipline, consistency, belief, or commitment. Responsibility increases, but authority does not. Effort escalates. Fatigue follows.

One reason self-help cannot resolve this pattern is that it assumes internal cooperation. It presumes that all parts of the self ultimately want improvement. But as earlier chapters have shown, some resistance does not want healing. It adapts to routines, exploits fatigue, and waits for effort to collapse. Self-help trains skills, but it does not confront opposition.

Constant improvement also produces continuous motion. Motion feels like progress. But motion without command does not restore authority. It prevents stillness. And stillness is often the condition in which intrusion becomes visible. In this way, self-help can unintentionally function as distraction—keeping the person busy while the deeper issue remains untouched.

Self-help culture also reframes failure in a damaging way. When methods fail, the person is told they did not apply them correctly or fully. The possibility that authority itself is compromised is rarely considered. The burden remains on the individual, while the underlying displacement remains unaddressed.

This chapter does not mock self-help. It defines its limit. Self-help can refine the self. It can strengthen habits, sharpen insight, and improve functioning. But refinement is not reclamation. For those experiencing internal displacement, improvement without authority becomes another form of management.

If self-help cannot restore command, many people turn next toward something that feels deeper, more meaningful, and more powerful. The following chapter examines why modern spirituality often provides comfort without authority—and why comfort without command leaves the core problem intact.

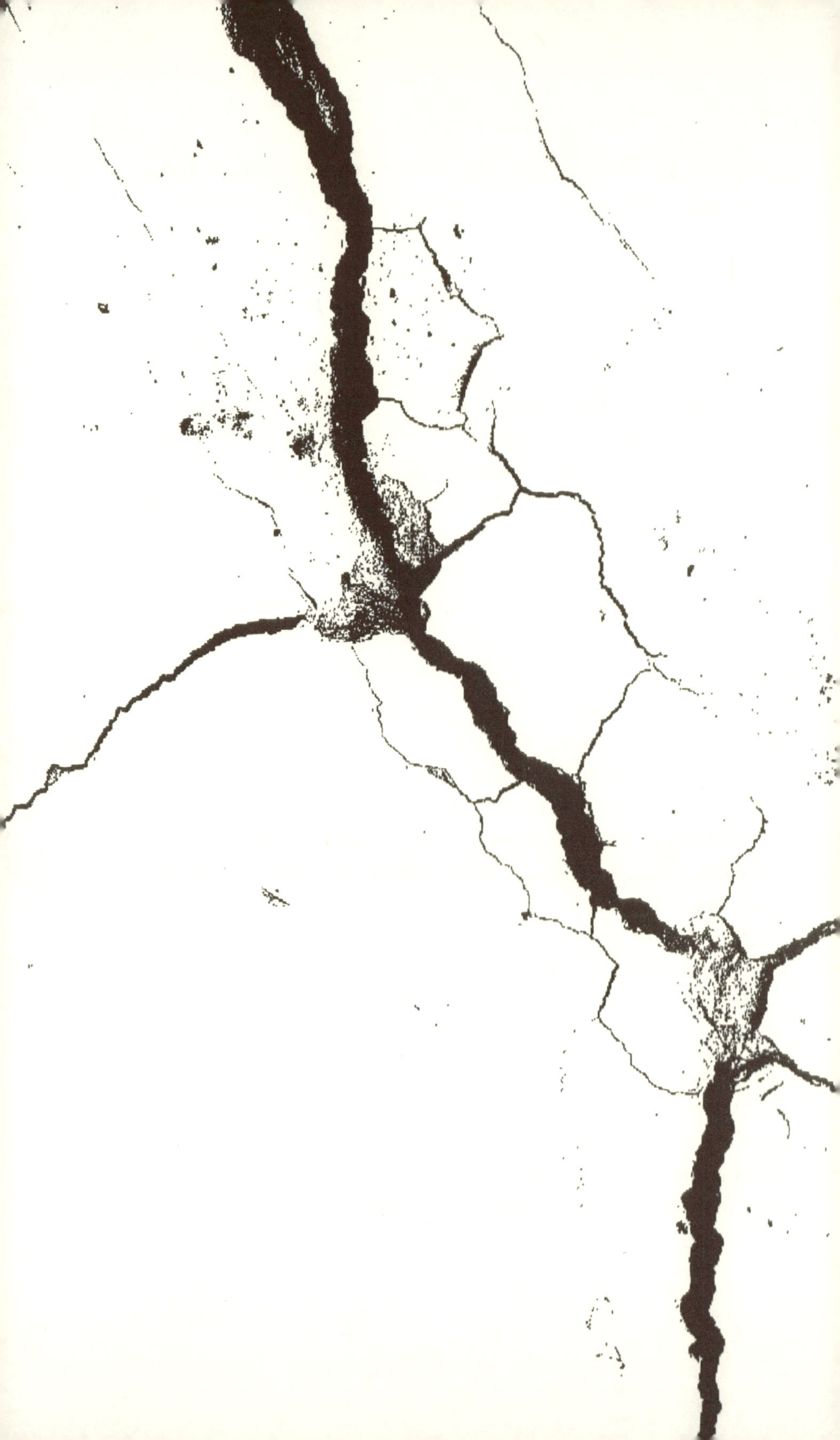

18

SPIRITUALITY WITHOUT POWER

When self-help fails to restore authority, many people turn toward spirituality. This shift often feels inevitable. The struggle no longer presents as purely behavioral or psychological; it feels deeper, harder to locate, more existential in nature. People sense that something is wrong beneath the surface of their thoughts and habits, something that cannot be solved through optimization alone. They begin searching for meaning, connection, and transcendence—hoping that what they cannot fix, they might somehow understand or soften.

That instinct is not misguided. It reflects an accurate perception that the problem is not merely technical. But the form spirituality most often takes in modern life is structurally ineffective for restoring authority.

Much of contemporary spirituality is designed to be comforting rather than confrontational. It avoids hierarchy, absolutes, and moral clarity. It favors language that soothes without demanding allegiance—energy, alignment, intention, vibration, shadow, growth. Nothing is named directly. Nothing is opposed explicitly. Nothing is commanded. This makes such spirituality widely acceptable, emotionally accessible, and socially safe. It also renders it powerless.

For a displaced self, this softness can feel like relief. Spiritual language reframes struggle as imbalance rather than conflict. It recasts resistance as a lesson, disruption as growth, and pressure as a signal to "lean in" rather than push back. Responsibility is softened. Opposition is neutralized through interpretation. The promise is harmony without resistance, healing without hierarchy, peace without command.

But gentleness is not authority. And harmony that avoids confrontation does not remove what opposes order.

Spirituality often succeeds where self-help fails by providing meaning. People feel seen. They feel connected to something larger than themselves. They feel less alone in their struggle. These are not trivial outcomes. Meaning matters. Orientation matters. But meaning is not mastery. A person can feel spiritually affirmed while remaining internally overridden. Connection does not equal command.

As this form of spirituality expands, one assumption quietly governs it: that nothing is truly wrong. Everything is reframed as part of a process. Every impulse is honored. Every experience is interpreted as necessary. Every path is valid. But when everything is valid, nothing has authority. There is no standard to defend, no boundary to enforce, and no enemy to resist. Opposition thrives in ambiguity.

This ambiguity is preserved through vague, symbolic language. Terms like ego, shadow, resistance, and blockage describe experience without assigning agency or responsibility. They allow endless exploration without decision. The struggle becomes something to observe rather than confront. Movement continues. Resolution does not.

One of the defining features of powerless spirituality is its refusal to name anything as adversarial. Everything is internal. Everything is symbolic. Everything is "part of the journey." But some resistance does not seek integration. It seeks access. And access is granted when nothing is opposed.

Ritual is often offered as the solution. Breathwork, meditation, visualization, affirmation, embodiment practices—these can calm the nervous system and provide temporary structure. They are not meaningless. But without authority, ritual becomes routine. Routine can be endured indefinitely. Authority must be obeyed. What does not recognize hierarchy cannot command compliance.

Many spiritual frameworks emphasize intention. Set your intention. Align your energy. Focus your thoughts. For certain challenges, intention helps. But intention without authority is fragile. A person can intend clarity and still be overridden. The will must be backed by power.

Powerless spirituality is attractive precisely because it demands nothing decisive. No allegiance. No submission. No renunciation. It allows a person to feel spiritually engaged without confronting control. This makes it safe. It also makes it ineffective.

Spirituality can orient the self. It can offer language, context, and comfort. But orientation is not liberation. Without authority, spirituality becomes another interpretive layer—another way to talk about the problem without removing it. Over time, comfort turns into complicity.

By refusing to name opposition, powerless spirituality inadvertently protects it. Nothing is challenged. Nothing is expelled. Nothing leaves. The person feels calmer—but remains occupied.

This chapter does not reject spirituality. It rejects spirituality without authority. The distinction matters. One restores order. The other maintains equilibrium. Only one confronts control.

If self-help refines but cannot reclaim, and spirituality comforts but cannot command, then the question becomes unavoidable: what actually defends the self?

19

WHAT A WILL IS (AND WHY IT FAILS)

Most people speak about the will as if it were identical to the self. They say, "I chose this," or "I didn't have the willpower," as though the will were a permanent engine that either functions well or poorly depending on character. In modern frameworks, the will is treated as an internal resource—something that can be strengthened, repaired, trained, or exhausted, but never fundamentally interrupted. That assumption is false.

The will is not the self, and it is not self-sustaining.

The will is a function—specifically, the function that authorizes action. It is the internal faculty that says now, that converts awareness into execution, that bridges knowing and doing. Without it, thoughts may occur, values may remain intact, and conscience may speak, but nothing initiates. This distinction matters because most explanations of captivity assume the will is always present. They assume people fail because they choose wrongly, resist insufficiently, or lack discipline. But these explanations collapse when confronted with one recurring experience: people often know exactly what is right—and cannot do it.

Not because they disagree.

Not because they desire otherwise.

But because the mechanism that authorizes action is not issuing commands.

The will is not infinite. It is not continuous. And it is not sovereign. The will operates under authority. This is not a religious claim. It is a structural one. The will does not generate its own legitimacy. It does not decide whether it has the right to command; it acts only when that right is intact. When authority is stable, the will functions effortlessly. When authority is compromised, the will becomes erratic, intermittent, or absent.

This is why people can endure immense pressure while remaining functional—and then suddenly break. The break is not moral. It is structural. The will has exceeded its capacity to authorize under load. Contrary to popular belief, willpower does not fail gradually. It does not weaken in smooth decline. It functions until it cannot—and then it stops. This is why people describe experiences of collapse as abrupt. One moment they are choosing; the next, they are reacting. One moment they are deciding; the next, they are watching themselves act.

This is not loss of consciousness. It is loss of command.

In these moments, the person is still present. They can observe. They can feel. They can even object internally. But objection without authorization is inert. The will is no longer issuing final orders. This is what most people mean—without the language to say it—when they say, "It's like something took over." They are not describing a new desire. They are describing the absence of authorization.

The will fails not because it is weak, but because it is not ultimate. It is a delegated authority, not an absolute one. It functions properly only when aligned under a higher order that grants it legitimacy. When that alignment collapses—through exhaustion, trauma, terror, dissociation, intoxication, prolonged overload, or deception—the will loses standing. And when standing is lost, something else fills the gap.

This is the part modern frameworks cannot explain because they deny the existence of vacancy. They assume the mind is always occupied by the self. But that assumption ignores a basic reality: a system without command does not remain neutral. Vacancy is not empty. It is an opening.

The will is not designed to operate alone. Humans are not sovereign entities. They are ordered beings, meant to function under authority rather than generate it independently. This does not negate free will; it explains its limits. Free will exists—but it exists under authority, not instead of it.

When people attempt to live as self-contained authorities, the will bears a load it was never meant to carry. Over time, it compensates through distraction, dissociation, or endurance. These are not moral failures. They are adaptive responses to overload. Distraction matters here—not as a cause of captivity, but as a stabilizer of it. People immerse themselves in games, scrolling, fantasy, or constant stimulation not because they want to lose control, but because these states suspend the need for authorization. When absorbed, the will is not required to initiate, decide, or resist. Momentum replaces command.

Isolation functions similarly. Humans borrow authority from shared reality. Relationship, accountability, and being seen reinforce internal command. Isolation removes these scaffolds. When the will is already strained, isolation leaves it unsupported. Again, not sinful—structural.

The critical moment arrives when strain exceeds capacity. At that moment, authorization fails. This is why possession can occur suddenly— not because nothing was happening before, but because the threshold was crossed. Authority does not degrade like habits do. It either holds or it collapses. And when it collapses, replacement is immediate.

This is why people experience possession as interruption. Thoughts are cut off. Reflection is preempted. Action occurs before consent is given. The person does not feel persuaded; they feel rushed. They do not feel convinced; they feel bypassed—because they are.

The will is no longer issuing commands.

I am not here to explain every mechanism. I am here to correct one false assumption: that consent precedes takeover. People assume control is only lost after permission is given. That assumption is false. What many describe is not agreement, curiosity, or invitation, but contact—a moment in which something asserts itself before the will can respond.

This book uses the word exposure not to soften the event, but to clarify it. Exposure does not imply cooperation. It describes impact. Just as the body does not consent to poison or force, the mind does not need to authorize intrusion in order for command to be displaced.

The takeover itself is immediate. What follows is adjustment—not progression.

This also explains why shame is such a poor explanatory tool. Shame assumes authorship. It assumes the will was present and chose wrongly.

But in occupation, the will was not present to choose at all. The person did not surrender values. They lost jurisdiction.

This is also why children are especially vulnerable. Children do not possess mature internal authority. They are governed externally by design. When trauma, terror, or violation occurs, displacement can happen immediately—not because the child invited anything, but because authority was never fully internalized. The will was not overridden. It had not yet fully formed.

This is not metaphor. It is structural reality.

Once the will has failed, it cannot restore itself. This is the most uncomfortable truth for modern people. We are taught that somewhere inside, the self remains fully intact, waiting to rise if we just try hard enough. But a compromised system cannot generate the authority required to reclaim itself. A prison does not generate its own exit.

This is why insight does not restore freedom. This is why courage does not return automatically. This is why people can see the truth clearly and remain trapped. Awareness does not authorize action. Only authority does.

And authority cannot arise from what has been displaced.

This is why the question of freedom is not primarily psychological, behavioral, or even moral. It is hierarchical. Who—or what—has the right to command when the will cannot?

Until that question is answered, every solution remains partial. Self-help refines. Psychology explains. Spirituality comforts. None restore command. The will does not need motivation. It needs rightful authority.

This is why occupation happens. Not because people want it. Not because they are weak. But because the human will is not self-sustaining. When authority is interrupted, vacancy appears. And vacancy is always filled.

Freedom is not restored by strengthening the will.

It is restored by reordering it under an authority that cannot be displaced.

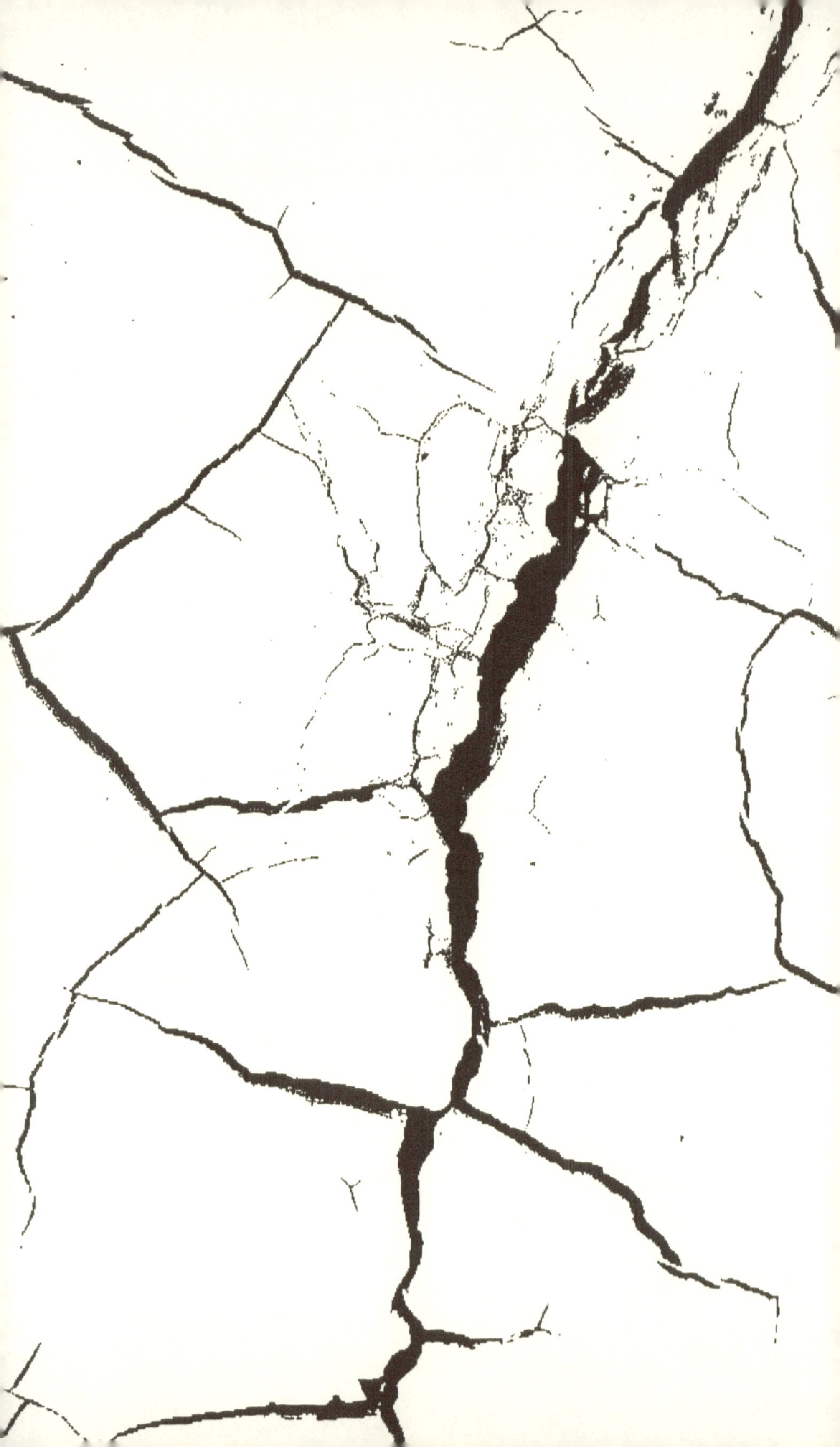

20

WHY SHAME IS THE ENEMY'S FAVORITE TOOL

Shame is not the same as guilt. Guilt says something I did was wrong. Shame says something I am is wrong. Guilt preserves agency. Shame destroys it. This is why shame is so effective in occupation.

After displacement occurs—whether suddenly or gradually—shame enters almost immediately. Not merely as an emotion, but as an explanation. People tell themselves that this must be their fault, that they must have wanted it, that they must be weak or broken. These conclusions feel moral, but they are not. They are corrosive.

Shame does not lead to repentance. It leads to collapse. It convinces the person that authority is permanently lost, that resistance is illegitimate, and that restoration is impossible. This is why shame appears after the takeover, not before. Before, the person resisted. After, shame explains why they no longer can.

Shame reframes displacement as identity. Instead of saying, "My authority was interrupted," the person says, "I am defective." This shift is devastating, because authority cannot be reclaimed if someone believes they never had the right to it in the first place.

Shame also keeps people silent. They do not speak because they assume exposure will confirm their worthlessness. They hide not because they are deceptive, but because they believe they are disqualified. This isolation deepens occupation—not because shame causes it, but because shame prevents challenge.

Another reason shame is so effective is that it feels like humility. People confuse self-condemnation with responsibility. They believe that harsh self-judgment proves moral seriousness. It does not. It proves authority has been reassigned. Conviction calls you forward. Shame pins you in place. Conviction says return. Shame says disappear.

This is why shame never produces lasting change. It may produce compliance, silence, or self-monitoring, but it does not produce restoration. In fact, shame often stabilizes occupation. Once a person believes they are fundamentally flawed, they stop expecting freedom. They adjust their goals downward. They settle for management instead of wholeness.

They say things like, "This is just how I am," or "I'll always struggle like this," or "I can't be trusted." These statements sound honest. They are concessions.

Shame also explains why people defend what harms them. If the system that displaced them is exposed as unjust, then their compliance becomes painful to acknowledge. Shame makes it easier to protect the system than to confront the loss. So shame redirects anger inward and keeps the real conflict hidden.

This is why shame must be confronted directly—not soothed, not reframed, but named. Shame is not evidence of moral awareness. It is evidence that authority has been displaced and redirected inward as self-attack.

This is why Jesus never uses shame to restore people. He names wrongdoing without erasing identity. He confronts without condemning. He restores authority by removing accusation. Because accusation is not corrective. It is paralyzing.

Until shame is removed, the self cannot stand upright again. And until the self can stand, authority cannot be exercised. This is why freedom often begins not with confidence, but with relief—relief that the problem was not who you are, relief that you were not disqualified, relief that authority can be restored.

Shame says you are the problem.

Truth says something happened to you.

Only one of those allows recovery.

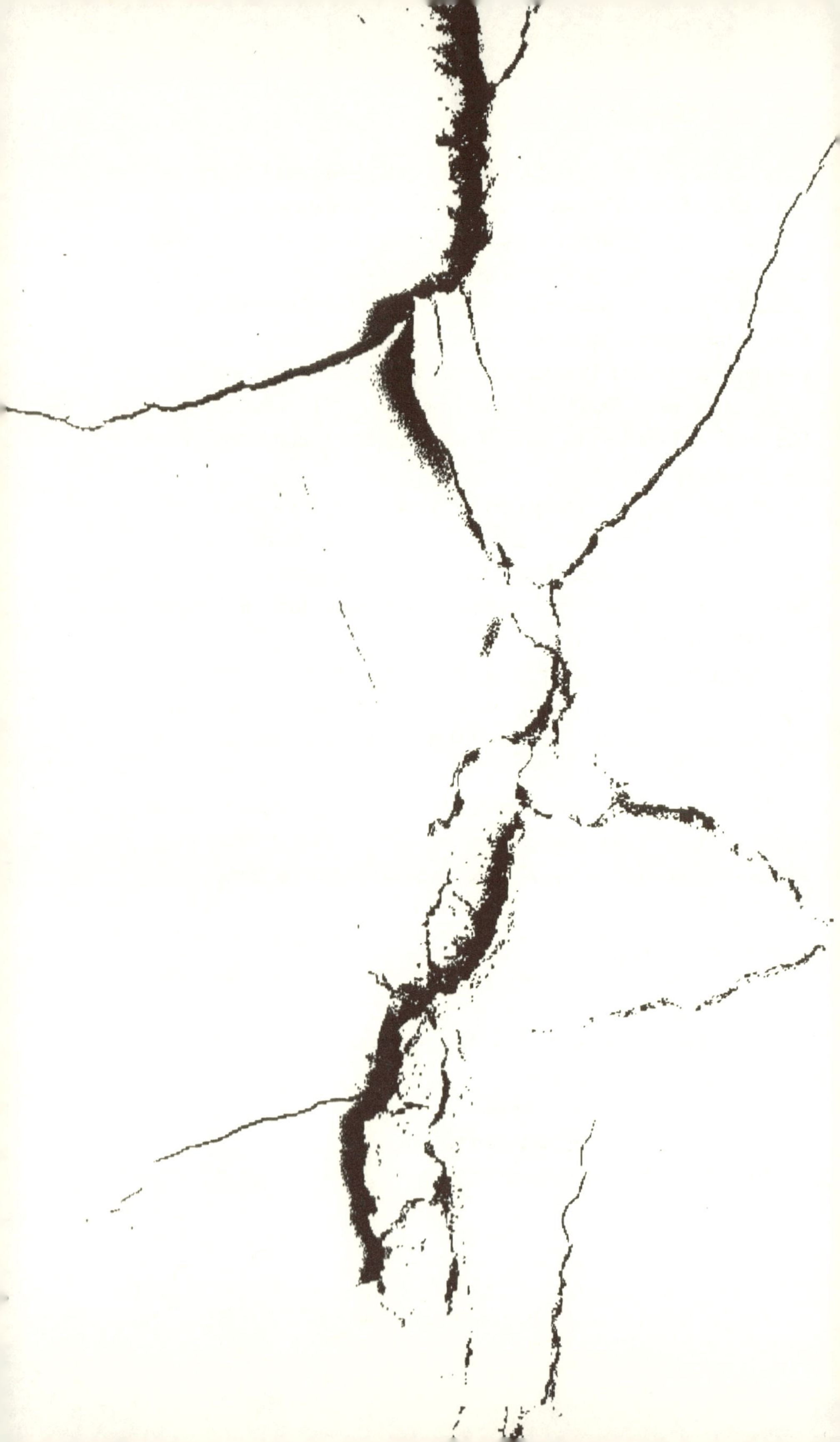

21

WHY POSSESSION CAN HAPPEN IN A MOMENT

One of the greatest misunderstandings about possession is the assumption that it always happens slowly. People are told it is a process of erosion, that it takes years, that it only comes after repeated choices, habits, or moral decline. Sometimes that is true. But not always.

Many people describe something very different. They say they were themselves—and then they weren't. That it happened suddenly. That it felt like a switch flipped. One moment everything was normal; the next, something was wrong.

These accounts are often dismissed because they do not fit modern frameworks. Psychology prefers gradual causation. Self-help prefers responsibility narratives. Spiritual language often defaults to ideas about "opening doors" through behavior. But these explanations fail to account for one undeniable fact: possession does not require persuasion. It requires access. And access can be granted in a moment.

What most explanations miss is an important distinction. The conditions that weaken internal authority may develop over time, but the takeover itself frequently occurs all at once. This is why people can function for years—holding jobs, raising families, making plans—and then experience a sudden internal rupture. They did not become a different person slowly. They lost command suddenly.

This does not mean nothing was happening before. It means authority does not collapse the way habits do. Authority is not eroded in degrees. It is either present—or it is not. And when it drops below a functional threshold, something else moves in immediately.

Afterward, people often search backward, trying to locate the cause. What did I do wrong? What did I invite? What choice caused this?

This search is understandable—but often misdirected. Possession does not require agreement. It does not require desire. It does not require intention. It requires a moment where the will is no longer governing.

That moment can come through extreme exhaustion, shock or trauma, intoxication or dissociation, terror or panic, surrender under pressure, the collapse of hope, overwhelming grief, or prolonged isolation followed by breaking strain. It can also come through deception itself. In these moments, the person does not choose anything. They cannot. The system that authorizes choice is offline.

And when authority drops out, vacancy appears. Vacancy is not neutral. When authority is absent, influence does not wait.

This is why the experience feels so violating afterward. People are often confused—not about what happened, but about how it happened. They say they didn't want this, didn't agree to this, that it goes against everything they believe. That is because it did not happen at the level of belief. It happened at the level of command.

The person did not surrender values. They lost jurisdiction. This is why guilt is such a poor explanation. Guilt assumes authorship. Possession involves displacement.

The person remains conscious. They remain aware. They remain morally intact. But the authority that normally governs thought, impulse, restraint, and action is no longer issuing the final directive. Something else is.

This is where gradual models fail. Gradual models work for habits, addictions, and character formation. They do not work for occupation. Occupation is not the strengthening of a pattern. It is the replacement of command.

This is why people say they don't recognize themselves anymore, that they know this isn't them, that they're watching themselves do things they would never choose. No amount of insight fixes this—because insight does not restore authority. You cannot reason your way back into a position you no longer hold.

One of the most damaging ideas people absorb is that possession only happens because someone invited it. This belief produces shame instead of clarity. It also ignores reality. People are possessed during accidents, surgeries, assaults, breakdowns, grief, prolonged illness, and states of collapse—moments where the will is compromised not morally, but structurally.

The person is not opening a door. The door disappears. And something steps into the space where command used to be.

This is especially important when considering children. Children do not possess mature internal authority. They are governed externally by design. This makes them more vulnerable—not because they are sinful, but because authority has not yet fully formed. This is why trauma, fear, or violation in childhood can result in sudden internal takeover. Not gradual conditioning. Immediate displacement.

The child does not choose. The child cannot resist. Authority was never fully theirs to begin with.

For many people, possession feels less like being controlled and more like being interrupted. They describe thoughts being cut off, an inability to finish a sentence internally, a sense of being rushed before they can decide, as if something steps in before they act. This is not coincidence.

Possession does not usually announce itself. It preempts. It blocks continuity between awareness and action. The person knows. The person sees. The person objects. But the objection never reaches execution—because execution requires authorization. And authorization no longer originates from the self.

Many people who experience sudden possession are not reckless, immoral, or undisciplined. They are often conscientious, sensitive, thoughtful, and responsible. They are people who endure long periods of pressure without relief. When they finally break, the break is mistaken for weakness. It is not. It is a structural failure under load.

And structural failure happens instantly.

This explains the depth of grief people feel afterward. They are not only grieving behavior. They are grieving authorship. They say they don't know where they went, that they feel like they disappeared, that they don't feel like themselves anymore. That grief is accurate. The self did not dissolve. It was displaced.

And displacement happens fast.

This matters for freedom. If possession only happened gradually, then effort, insight, and habit change would be sufficient. But because possession can occur in a moment, freedom must be restored at the level of authority—not behavior. You do not undo a coup with self-reflection. You restore command.

This is why the solution cannot come from the compromised system itself. And this is why people who experience sudden possession often know—instinctively—that the answer must come from outside them. Not because they are weak, but because they are accurate.

Possession does not mean you failed.

It does not mean you wanted it.

It does not mean you invited it.

It means authority was interrupted.

And interruption does not require consent.

It requires vulnerability.

This is why sudden possession is not a contradiction of gradual influence. It is its outcome. Preparation can be slow. But occupation is immediate.

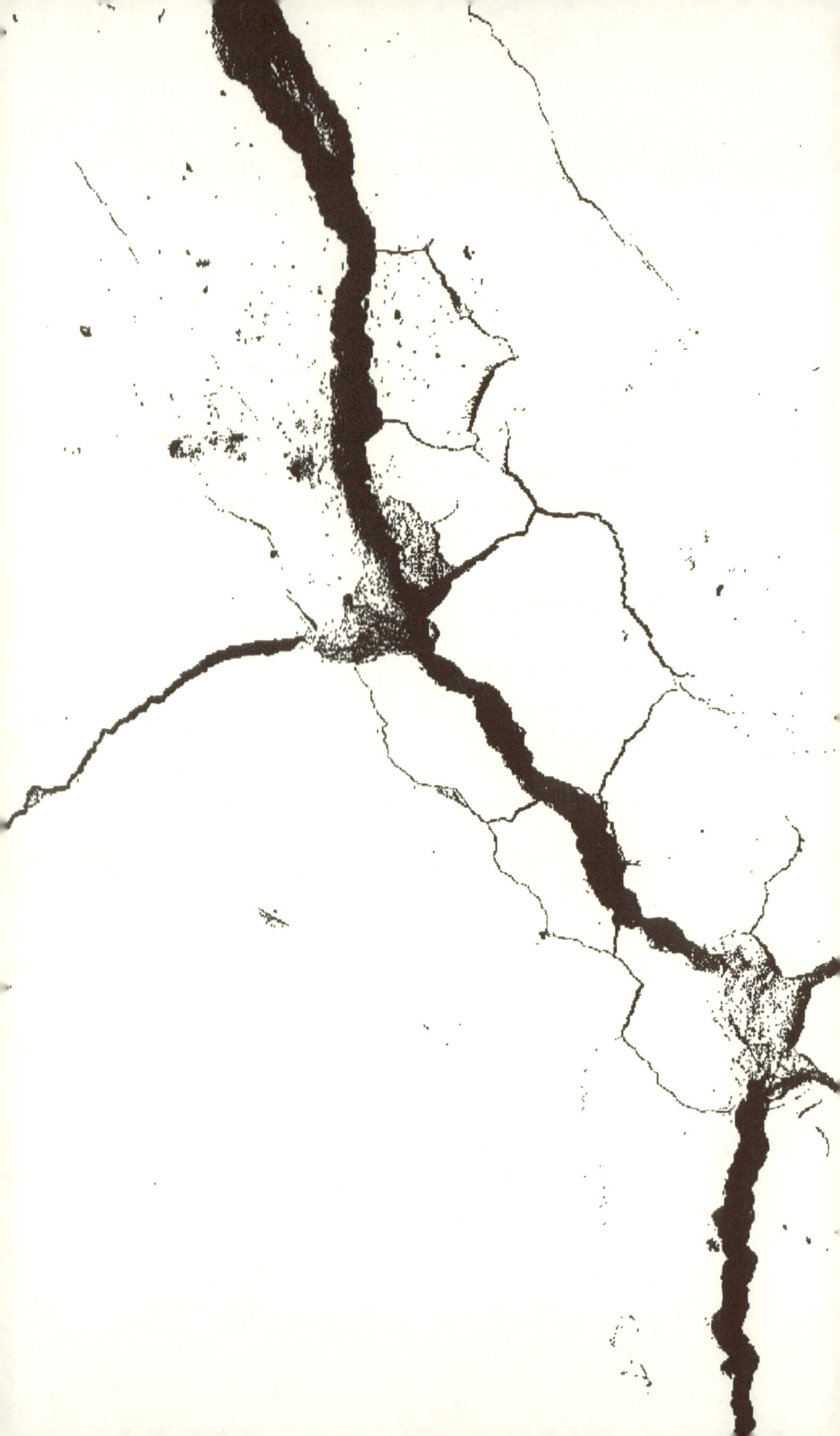

22

WHY SOME PEOPLE SENSE THE SHIFT IMMEDIATELY

One of the most confusing aspects of occupation is how unevenly it is experienced. Some people know immediately that something is wrong. They feel it before they can explain it. They may still function, still perform, still appear intact—but internally, they are alarmed. Others live for years without that recognition. They adapt, cope, and explain things away. They do not feel "right," but they also do not feel overtly invaded.

This difference often leads to misunderstanding. Those who sense the shift early wonder why others do not see it. Those who do not sense it assume the early-aware are exaggerating, overthinking, or unstable. Neither conclusion is accurate.

The difference is not intelligence, morality, weakness, or strength. It is what the person is oriented to internally. Some people are oriented primarily to comfort, performance, or external stability. Others are oriented to coherence, integrity, and internal authority. When authority shifts, the second group feels it immediately.

They may not know what happened or have language for it, but they know something essential is out of place—not because life stopped working, but because they did. These individuals often say they do not feel like themselves anymore, that they cannot locate themselves internally, or that something feels off at the center. What they are sensing is not emotion. It is loss of command.

People who are attuned to inner authority notice when it disappears the way someone notices when gravity changes. Nothing external has to collapse. The disruption is internal and immediate. This sensitivity is frequently misdiagnosed. Modern frameworks label it as anxiety, hypervigilance, or over-identification with thoughts. In reality, it is often the opposite.

These individuals are not obsessed with their inner world. They are anchored to it. They rely on continuity between thought, conscience, and action to function. When that continuity breaks, they feel disoriented even if nothing dramatic has occurred.

By contrast, people who are externally oriented can lose internal authority without immediate distress. They borrow structure from routines, roles, relationships, and expectations. As long as those remain intact, the absence of inner command is less noticeable. They are not less affected. They are less aware.

This explains why some people appear to "fall apart" quickly while others seem stable for years. The early-aware person is not weaker; they are less buffered. The buffered person is not stronger; they are more scaffolded. Both are vulnerable. They simply register the loss differently.

Early awareness is often isolating. The person senses displacement before they have language for it, before anyone else sees a problem, and before there is permission to speak. They may be told they are tired, overthinking, or need to relax. But what they are experiencing is not stress. It is misalignment.

They are still present, conscious, and morally intact. But the internal signal that says this is me, this is mine, this is under my authority has weakened or disappeared. Because they rely on that signal to navigate life, its absence is immediate and alarming.

This early sensing is not pathology. It is detection. It does not mean the person is closer to collapse; it means they are closer to truth. Unfortunately, because modern culture does not recognize loss of internal authority as a category, early-aware individuals are often taught to distrust their own perception. They learn to override the signal, normalize the absence, and function without authorship.

Over time, they may lose the very sensitivity that warned them—not because it was wrong, but because it was inconvenient.

Understanding this difference matters. It prevents comparison, shame, and false conclusions about who is "doing worse." Some people feel occupation early because they are oriented to coherence. Others feel it late because they are oriented to survival.

Neither orientation caused the occupation.

But one makes it visible sooner.

23

MORAL RELATIVISM AND THE LOSS OF DEFENSE

very system of defense depends on distinction. Something must be identified as acceptable, and something must be rejected. Without that separation, no boundary can hold. Moral relativism removes this separation. It teaches that good and evil are subjective, situational, or socially constructed; that harm is a matter of perspective; that restraint is preference; and that judgment itself is a form of oppression.

At first, this feels humane. Over time, it leaves the self undefended.

Modern culture often treats moral certainty as a threat. Conviction is labeled rigidity. Boundaries are labeled intolerance. Judgment is labeled harm. As a result, people are encouraged to soften every line until nothing is clearly wrong, nothing is firmly right, and everything depends. But defense does not operate on ambiguity.

Moral boundaries do not exist to shame. They exist to protect. They define what is permitted, what is resisted, and what is rejected. Without these distinctions, the self cannot say no with authority. And when the self cannot say no, influence does not need to argue.

Tolerance has value in social life. But when tolerance replaces discernment internally, it becomes dangerous. Every impulse is entertained. Every desire is explored. Every resistance is questioned. The person no longer asks whether something is good. They ask who they are to judge.

That question sounds humble. It is also disarming.

Influence thrives where opposition is illegitimate. If nothing can be named as wrong, nothing can be confronted. If every force is reframed as a part of the self, no force can be expelled. Relativism does not remove power struggles. It removes the language required to resist them.

When external moral structures dissolve, inner law must compensate. But relativism undermines inner law as well. Conscience is reframed as conditioning. Conviction is reframed as bias. Restraint is reframed as repression. The self is left without a standard it can defend without apology.

Within a relativistic framework, guilt has no clear function. If nothing is truly wrong, why does guilt persist? People are taught to reinterpret guilt as shame, trauma, or social programming. Sometimes this is accurate. But when guilt signals real misalignment, dismissing it removes guidance. The alarm sounds, and it is silenced.

Non-judgment is often presented as wisdom. But judgment is not condemnation. It is evaluation. A self that cannot evaluate cannot protect itself. Non-judgment internally creates openness without hierarchy—everything is allowed to pass through.

This is not freedom. It is exposure.

One of the most significant consequences of moral relativism is the removal of the word evil from serious conversation. The term is considered extreme, outdated, or inflammatory. So it is replaced with softer language—dysfunction, maladaptation, coping, imbalance. These words describe behavior. They do not oppose it.

To resist something consistently, the self must believe resistance is justified. Not optional. Not situational. Not symbolic. Justified. Moral relativism removes that confidence. The person hesitates, second-guesses, and accommodates. Influence proceeds unchallenged.

In exchange for moral neutrality, people receive social approval. They avoid conflict. They appear tolerant. They feel modern. But the trade is costly. Without moral clarity, the self loses its shield.

This chapter does not argue for cruelty or rigidity. It argues for clarity. Clarity allows compassion without confusion, boundaries without hatred, and resistance without shame. Without clarity, compassion collapses into permissiveness.

When inner authority is weakened, when self-help substitutes for command, and when spirituality avoids power, moral relativism removes the final line of defense. Nothing remains to say, This does not belong here.

Up to this point, the book has shown what fails: self-help without authority, spirituality without power, and morality without clarity. The next section asks a more difficult question. If defense requires authority, where does that authority come from?

The next chapter begins that inquiry not with answers, but with a constraint: you cannot evict what you cannot command.

Most people assume that seeing the truth is the hard part—that once misalignment is recognized, the rest will follow naturally. They believe clarity leads to change and awareness restores agency. But awareness alone does not undo occupation.

In fact, awareness often arrives after the structures that sustain the problem are already in place. People can see that their lives no longer reflect who they are and still remain inside them. They can name the compromises, recognize the drift, and yet not understand how it happened.

Nothing moves. Nothing changes.

This is not weakness. Awareness does not remove consequences. By the time someone becomes fully conscious of what has happened, their life is already built around it. Relationships depend on compliance. Income relies on silence. Stability is tied to staying put. Awareness reveals the truth and, simultaneously, the cost of acting on it.

That cost feels overwhelming. Change would require disruption, loss, uncertainty, and a redefinition of self. So awareness transforms into something else. It becomes observation without movement.

People learn how to live with knowing. They carry recognition quietly, adjust expectations, and tell themselves they will address it later. Awareness becomes a private burden rather than a catalyst. Over time, even that awareness dulls—not because the truth disappears, but because holding it without action is unsustainable.

This is why people remain in lives they can clearly describe as wrong. Not because they do not see. But because seeing does not automatically restore the power to leave.

Awareness exposes the fracture. It does not heal it. And until something interrupts the system that holds a person in place, awareness alone will deepen the ache without changing the outcome.

THE QUESTION OF AUTHORITY

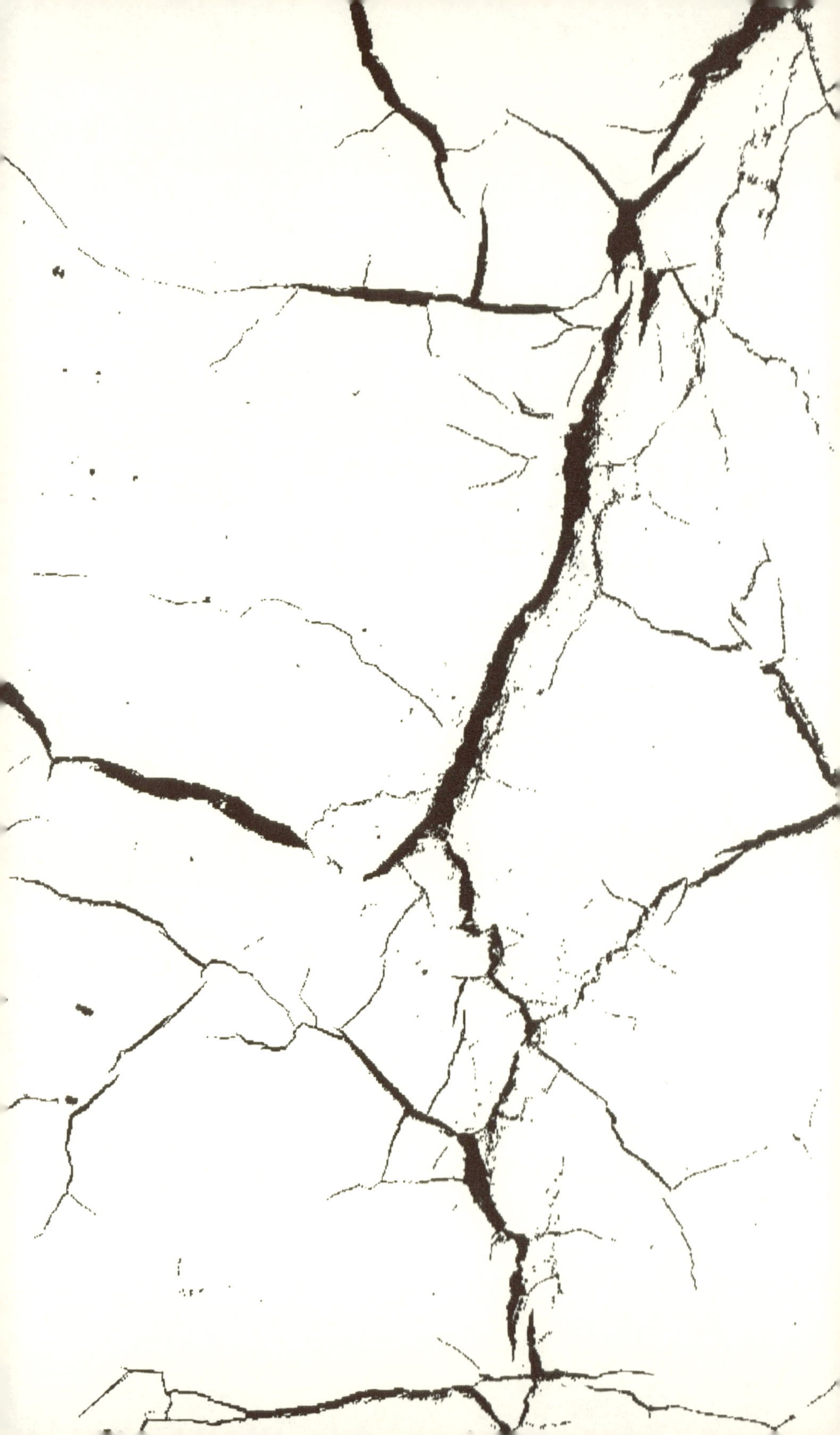

24

YOU CANNOT EVICT WHAT YOU CANNOT COMMAND

Every serious attempt at freedom eventually runs into the same wall. The person understands the pattern, recognizes the opposition, and wants change—and yet nothing leaves. At this point, effort intensifies. Discipline increases. Insight deepens. Boundaries are attempted. Still, the internal pressure remains.

This is where most people become exhausted and confused, because removal requires something effort cannot supply. Effort is an action of the will. But the will is already compromised. Telling a displaced self to try harder assumes the very authority that has been lost. It places responsibility on a system that no longer governs itself.

This is why effort so often backfires. The more the person strains, the more resistance they encounter. The struggle becomes internal warfare—loud, draining, and inconclusive. Many people confuse authority with intensity. They assume that if they are forceful enough—disciplined enough, motivated enough, committed enough—control will return.

But authority is not volume. It is position.

Authority does not argue, plead, or negotiate. It commands, and it is obeyed.

Earlier chapters emphasized naming the problem. Naming is necessary, but it is insufficient. You can name an intruder and still be powerless to remove it. Recognition does not equal command. This is why many people reach a point where they say, "I know what this is—but I still can't stop it." They are correct.

Modern frameworks often suggest that removal happens internally: you reframe, integrate, outgrow, or release. These methods assume cooperation. But eviction requires hierarchy. Something must have the right to issue a final order. Without that right, nothing leaves.

Negotiation assumes shared interest. But the forces described throughout this book do not share the person's interest in wholeness, clarity, or freedom. They benefit from fragmentation, exhaustion, and confusion. Negotiation strengthens them because it acknowledges legitimacy where none exists.

When a person attempts to confront opposition using their own compromised will, they approach it as an equal—two voices, two arguments, no final authority. This results in endless internal dialogue: insight without resolution. Authority ends dialogue.

Boundaries are declarations, and declarations require enforcement. A boundary without authority is a request, and requests can be ignored. This is why people say, "I set boundaries—but they don't hold." The boundary exists. The power to enforce it does not.

Many people arrive at this truth through exhaustion. They have tried everything that depends on self-command and failed. They are not lazy, uncommitted, or unwilling. They are outmatched. This realization is not despair. It is clarity.

Freedom begins with an admission most modern people resist: the self cannot always free itself. This is not weakness. It is accuracy. And accuracy restores orientation.

Authority cannot arise from what has been displaced. A compromised system cannot generate the power needed to reclaim itself. Authority must come from outside the hierarchy that has been overtaken. This is not mystical. It is structural.

This chapter does not yet identify the source of authority. It establishes the requirement. Before anything can be removed, something with the right to command must be present. Without that, every attempt at freedom becomes management.

The question is no longer whether authority is needed. It is whose authority counts.

The next chapter confronts a paradox modern culture avoids: every freedom requires allegiance, because command does not exist in a vacuum.

People often assume that once the truth is seen, courage will follow— that awareness will accumulate until it finally tips into action, that clarity strengthens resolve, that time restores bravery. But courage does not work that way inside captivity.

Courage is not a feeling, confidence, or the absence of fear. Courage is an act of authority. It requires an internal command that says move—a directive that overrides risk, consequence, and resistance. When that command no longer originates from the self, courage cannot simply reappear.

This is why waiting does not work. People tell themselves they will speak when they feel stronger, leave when they feel ready, act when the moment feels right. But readiness never arrives—not because the person is avoiding action, but because courage cannot regenerate inside a system that has displaced the will.

Time does not restore what time did not break. Habits deepen. Structures harden. The cost of action increases. Each day that passes without movement reinforces the same internal message: action is not authorized.

People may still admire courage in others. They may even long for it. But longing is not capacity. They watch others act decisively and feel something tighten—not inspiration, but distance. That's not me anymore.

This is the quiet lie captivity produces—not that courage is unnecessary, but that it is no longer accessible.

So people adapt. They redefine courage as endurance, patience, or staying put. They tell themselves they are being strong by surviving, tolerating, and carrying the weight without complaint. But endurance without agency is not courage. It is compliance reframed as virtue.

This is why encouragement often backfires. Telling someone to "be brave" assumes bravery is available on demand. It speaks to a self that no longer holds command. Instead of empowering, it deepens shame—because the person already knows what should be done and cannot do it.

The truth is simple and severe: courage does not return on its own because courage requires a sovereign will. And the will has been displaced.

Until authority is restored from outside the occupied system, courage will remain admired, envied, even mourned—but not enacted. This is not a moral failure. It is a structural one.

And no amount of waiting will reverse it.

25

EVERY FREEDOM REQUIRES A HIGHER ALLEGIANCE

Modern culture treats freedom as independence. To be free is to answer to no one. To be autonomous is to be ungoverned. To be empowered is to owe nothing. This sounds liberating. It is also impossible.

No one lives without allegiance. Every person serves something—whether they name it or not. Time. Desire. Approval. Comfort. Impulse. Fear. The question is not whether you are governed. It is by what.

Authority flows from allegiance. What you submit to has the right to command you. What you obey shapes what you become. When allegiance is fragmented, authority weakens. When allegiance is denied, authority disappears. The self cannot command itself in a vacuum. It must be ordered under something higher than impulse.

Submission is one of the most avoided words in modern life. It is associated with weakness, loss, and coercion. It is framed as the opposite of freedom. But this framing ignores reality.

Every system requires order. Every order requires hierarchy. Every hierarchy requires allegiance. Without these, power does not vanish. It relocates.

Many people believe they are free because they have not chosen an allegiance. In truth, they have simply defaulted to one. They obey whatever is loudest, whatever is most urgent, whatever offers relief. This is not freedom. It is reactivity.

Influence thrives where allegiance is undefined. When nothing higher governs the self, impulses compete freely. The strongest wins—not because it is right, but because it is unchecked. This is why opposition resists clarity. Clarity forces alignment. Alignment exposes allegiance.

Not all allegiance is enslaving. There is a difference between submission that restores order and submission that erases agency. One strengthens the self. The other consumes it.

The key distinction is this: true authority returns the will. False authority replaces it.

This is the paradox modern culture avoids. Freedom is not the absence of limits. It is the presence of the right limits. A musician is free because they submit to structure. A language speaker is free because they submit to grammar. A disciplined mind is free because it submits to truth. Constraint, when rightly ordered, produces power.

Many people arrive at this realization through exhaustion. They have tried to govern themselves without reference to anything higher. They have trusted desire. They have trusted reason. They have trusted emotion. They have trusted identity. None held. The self became fragmented under the strain.

To submit to rightful authority is not to disappear. It is to be re-centered. The self regains position by aligning with something that cannot be displaced. This alignment restores hierarchy. Hierarchy restores command.

If freedom requires allegiance, then neutrality is not an option. Every refusal to choose becomes a choice by default. So the question is no longer philosophical. It is practical:

What—or who—has the authority to command what opposes you?

This chapter does not yet answer that question. It establishes the condition. Authority must stand higher than the self, speak without ambiguity, possess the capacity to command, and be recognized by that which resists. Without these, allegiance is symbolic—and symbolism cannot evict opposition.

The next chapter addresses why naming the enemy matters, and what happens when the struggle is finally spoken plainly. Because confrontation does not begin with effort. It begins with recognition.

Freedom is often imagined as relief. But for people who have lived a long time inside misalignment, freedom does not feel light. It feels destabilizing. By the time awareness arrives, a person's life is already structured around the very things that restrict them. Their routines depend on it. Their relationships expect it. Their sense of belonging is tied to it.

So when the possibility of change appears, it does not register as opportunity. It registers as danger. Freedom threatens continuity. It threatens the roles people are known for, the expectations others rely on, the version of themselves that keeps things running smoothly.

Leaving misalignment would require explaining, confronting, and disappointing. It would require becoming unfamiliar—not just to others, but to themselves. That unfamiliarity feels risky.

People do not fear freedom because they love captivity. They fear it because freedom removes predictability. It demands decisions without a script. It asks them to tolerate uncertainty. It forces them to live without the protections they have built.

Even pain can become familiar. And familiarity feels safer than the unknown. So freedom gets reframed. It is labeled irresponsible, impractical, selfish. People tell themselves they are being realistic—that now is not the right time, that others depend on them, that stability matters more.

Sometimes those concerns are real. But underneath them is fear—not fear of failure, but fear of disintegration. Because if they step out of the life they have been maintaining, they do not yet know who they will be on the other side.

Freedom requires identity to be rebuilt, not just reclaimed. And rebuilding feels overwhelming when the self has been quiet for so long. So people stay—not because they do not want freedom, but because freedom would force them to confront how much of their life has been constructed without it.

And that reckoning feels heavier than the confinement itself.

26

WHY NAMING THE ENEMY MATTERS

Avoidance often disguises itself as wisdom. People hesitate to name what opposes them because naming feels extreme, divisive, or dangerous. So they soften their language, generalize their experience, and keep things abstract, relying on terms that feel safer, less confrontational, and easier to live with. This caution feels reasonable, even responsible, but unnamed opposition cannot be confronted.

Throughout this book, a pattern has been traced—not theorized or dramatized, but observed. The pattern is consistent: loss of agency, intrusive thought, erosion of authority, aversion to truth and stillness, compulsion defended as choice, and self-sabotage that restores fragmentation. These are not random symptoms. They do not appear independently or resolve on their own. They behave with coherence, escalating when challenged, retreating when ignored, and returning when authority weakens. Coherence implies intent.

Modern frameworks resist this conclusion. They prefer neutrality, describing processes rather than agency and dynamics rather than direction. They explain endlessly while avoiding moral or adversarial language. In doing so, they erase responsibility, intention, and opposition from the discussion entirely. This is not accidental. To name an enemy is to admit conflict, and to admit conflict is to require a side. Neutrality dissolves obligation.

When opposition is softened into euphemism, it gains cover. "Intrusive thoughts" sound manageable. "Coping behaviors" sound adaptive. "Resistance" sounds temporary. But what persists, adapts, and retaliates is not neutral. Language that minimizes threat also minimizes response. When something is framed as impersonal, it is treated as unavoidable; when it is framed as internal, it is endured; when it is framed as normal, it is accommodated. Accommodation strengthens what should be resisted.

One of the clearest indicators of adversarial influence is its reaction to exposure. Naming provokes pushback. Discomfort intensifies, confusion increases, and doubt surges. The person feels an almost immediate temptation to retreat into vagueness again—to soften the language, reconsider, or tell themselves they are being dramatic or unbalanced. This reaction is not incidental. Exposure threatens access.

At the same time, naming must be precise. Misnaming is as dangerous as silence. Blaming the self produces shame. Blaming the past produces paralysis. Blaming culture produces helplessness. None of these restore command. They redirect attention without restoring authority, leaving the problem active while responsibility is misassigned.

Naming an enemy is not the same as assigning blame. Blame collapses responsibility; discernment restores it. Discernment says that something is not the self, does not belong, and does not have authority here. Without discernment, everything is internalized—and nothing is resisted.

When opposition is named accurately, something reorganizes. Confusion clarifies, self-blame loosens, and authority begins to realign. The person stops asking what is wrong with them and begins asking what is acting against them. This shift is subtle, but decisive.

Many people avoid naming opposition because they fear it will increase distress. In practice, the opposite is often true. Uncertainty exhausts, ambiguity destabilizes, and endless analysis drains. Clarity stabilizes. Even when the truth is uncomfortable, it restores footing. It gives the mind something solid to stand on and replaces endless internal negotiation with orientation.

Naming is not the end of the struggle, but it is the beginning of resistance. It draws a boundary and declares that what is acting is not internal, not neutral, and not something to be negotiated with. This is how authority is positioned correctly—not because naming itself removes influence, but because it allows authority to be applied where it belongs.

Up to this point, this book has restored clarity. What comes next restores hope—but not false hope. The way out does not begin with belief; it begins with exhaustion. When nothing else works, people finally become open to authority they did not previously consider. The next chapter examines that moment, not as failure, but as readiness.

PART 7

THE WAY OUT

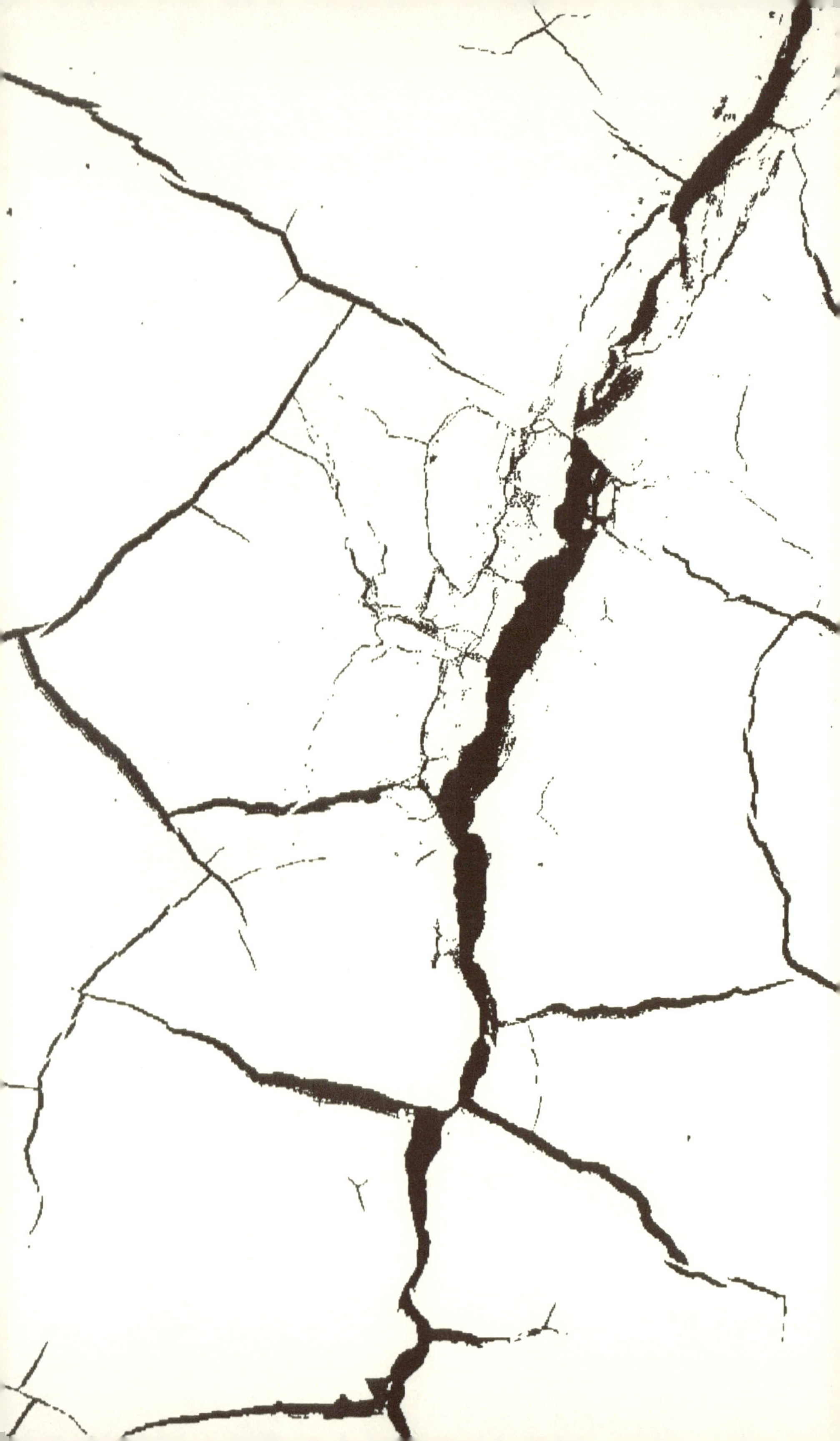

27

WHEN NOTHING ELSE WORKS

There is a point where people stop asking whether something is wrong and start organizing their lives around managing it. They do not resolve the problem; they accommodate it. They adjust routines, avoid certain topics, lower expectations of themselves, and create explanations that make the experience survivable. This feels like adaptation. From the outside, it looks like resilience. From the inside, it feels like relief.

The tension decreases. The questions quiet. The urgency fades. And that fading is often mistaken for healing. But what has actually happened is stabilization. The system has learned how to function with the intrusion intact. This is one of the most dangerous stages, because nothing appears to be deteriorating anymore. The chaos of earlier stages gives way to something that feels sustainable.

People are no longer constantly distressed. They are no longer searching desperately. They are no longer naming the problem as loudly. They are coping. But coping is not the same as freedom. Coping assumes the condition is permanent. It accepts limitation as the new baseline and focuses on reducing discomfort rather than restoring authority. The self no longer expects wholeness—only manageability.

This is why people often say things like they've learned to live with it, that it's just how their mind works now, or that everyone struggles like this. These statements are not neutral observations. They are concessions. And concessions, once normalized, harden into structure.

The self reorganizes around avoidance rather than agency. Energy is spent maintaining equilibrium instead of confronting what disrupted it. Life becomes about not making things worse. At this stage, resistance feels irresponsible. Questioning the arrangement threatens the fragile balance that has been achieved. Disturbing it risks reopening pain, confusion, or instability. So people protect the system—not because it is good, but because it is familiar. They mistake stability for safety.

But safety that requires surrender is not safety at all. It is containment. And there is another sign that this authority has been displaced—one that many people live inside for years without naming. There is a stage where identity stops feeling like something you inhabit and starts feeling like something you maintain.

People no longer experience themselves directly. They monitor themselves. They track reactions, measure tone, and adjust posture, language, and expression. They ask quietly whether something is acceptable, safe, or expected. And because these adjustments happen gradually, they do not feel artificial. They feel responsible.

Identity becomes functional. People learn which parts of themselves are useful and which parts create friction. They keep what works and minimize the rest—not because they want to be fake, but because friction has become costly. Over time, the self is reorganized around performance.

They still recognize themselves in pieces. They still feel familiar in certain moments. But the experience of being fully present inside their own life fades. They are always slightly outside themselves, watching. This is not self-awareness. It is self-management.

They become careful with opinions, careful with emotion, and careful with honesty. They are not lying—they are editing. And because editing is often praised as maturity, restraint, or professionalism, the loss goes unnoticed. People are rewarded for being manageable, predictable, agreeable, and low-maintenance.

So the internal system adapts. The self learns not to emerge spontaneously, not to take initiative without checking the environment first, and not to exist without permission. This is how identity becomes conditional. The person does not feel erased. They feel contained. And containment feels safer than disappearance.

But containment comes with a cost. The range of self-expression narrows. Emotional depth flattens. Creative impulse dulls. People stop surprising themselves. They rely on rehearsed responses, established roles, and predictable versions of who they are. Life becomes navigable—but thin. They do not feel broken. They feel managed.

This is why many people struggle to articulate what feels wrong. They can point to stress, fatigue, or burnout, but the deeper loss is harder to name. They are no longer living from the inside out. They are maintaining a version of themselves that fits. And because that version functions—pays bills, keeps relationships intact, avoids disruption—there is no obvious reason to question it.

Until moments break through. A flash of grief when remembering who they used to be. A quiet resentment toward people who seem free. A dull ache that surfaces in stillness. These moments feel intrusive and inconvenient, so they are managed too. People distract themselves, stay busy, and rationalize. They tell themselves this is adulthood, responsibility, real life.

But responsibility does not require self-erasure. And real life does not require constant self-monitoring. When identity becomes something you manage instead of live, something fundamental has shifted. The self is no longer the source. It is the product. And products exist to meet expectations—not to exercise authority.

This is one of the clearest signs that occupation has moved beyond influence and into structure. Because the self is no longer acting. It is being maintained. People stop saying something is wrong and start saying this is complicated. They stop saying they want out and start saying they're working through it. They stop imagining restoration and start managing symptoms.

The system benefits enormously from this shift. Because a person who is coping is no longer looking for rescue. They are no longer expecting intervention. They are no longer questioning authority. They are focused on maintenance. And maintenance keeps everything in place.

This is why breakthrough rarely comes during the coping phase. Not because the person is unwilling, but because they have adjusted to life without expecting their will to be fully restored. They have learned how to survive without sovereignty. That adaptation feels like progress. But it is actually the final stabilization of takeover.

And once stabilization sets in, the system no longer needs to exert pressure. The person is carrying it for them. There is a point where people stop merely tolerating what confines them and begin defending it—not because it is good and not because they are free to leave, but because it has become the structure that keeps them functional.

By the time occupation is complete, the ability to initiate resistance has already been compromised. What remains is not choice, but adaptation. Once a life is built around misalignment, anything that threatens that structure feels like a threat to survival itself, so people protect it.

They push back when it's questioned. They bristle when others speak clearly. They feel strangely irritated by anyone who refuses to comply in the same ways they did. This reaction is not conscious or deliberate. It is stabilization.

When exit is no longer perceived as possible, the mind reorganizes to reduce pain inside the enclosure. This defense is not evidence of freedom. It is evidence that resistance no longer originates inside the will itself.

People tell themselves they're being realistic, balanced, and reasonable. But what they are actually protecting is not the system—it is the cost they already paid to remain inside it. Because if the system is exposed as harmful, then staying within it becomes harder to survive psychologically.

If someone else speaks with clarity and walks away, it introduces a comparison the captive self cannot process—not because it disagrees, but because it cannot follow. So clarity becomes destabilizing. People reinterpret it as arrogance, judgment, or naivety, not because those labels are accurate, but because clarity threatens the internal equilibrium that now keeps everything from collapsing.

This is how people appear loyal to what diminished them. They align with rules they don't respect, defend structures that drained them, and repeat arguments they don't fully believe—not because they are convinced, but because dismantling the structure would require confronting losses they are no longer able to carry.

Defense becomes reflexive. They do not ask whether the system is right. They ask whether questioning it is dangerous. And when danger is perceived, defense follows automatically.

This is why people can appear passionate about lives that hollow them out—why they argue hardest for choices they secretly resent and lash out at anyone who reminds them of another way. They are not protecting the truth. They are protecting themselves from the collapse that would follow if the truth were fully faced without the power to act on it.

As long as the will remains displaced, the system stays intact—not because it is strong, but because the captive mind has learned how to survive inside it.

There is a moment many people recognize but struggle to explain. It begins with a rational thought that is not dramatic or revolutionary, just a quiet recognition that they don't want to keep doing this, that this isn't who they are, that they always regret it afterward. The thought forms clearly enough to be felt, but not long enough to be examined.

Before it can develop, something cuts in. The mind shifts. Attention diverts. Urgency replaces reflection. The thought dissolves, and the familiar pattern resumes. People often describe this as weakness, lack of discipline, or self-sabotage. But what's happening is not failure of reason. It is interruption.

The mind does not allow the thought to continue long enough to produce change. The recognition appears and is immediately neutralized—not argued against, not disproven, simply cut off. This is one of the most frustrating aspects of captivity because it mimics choice. People feel as though they almost acted differently.

They feel close to clarity but never able to stay there. The thought never reaches planning, decision, or execution. It dies at inception. And because the interruption happens internally, it feels self-generated. People blame themselves. They say they knew better, ask why they did it again, and conclude they always do this.

But the deeper question—when they will live as themselves again—is continually deferred. What they don't see is that the system never allowed the thought to mature into action. Rational processing requires time. It requires holding discomfort long enough to examine consequences, sustained attention, and the ability to remain present while tension builds.

In captivity, sustained attention is precisely what is blocked. The moment a thought threatens the established pattern, the system reacts. Distraction appears. Compulsion intensifies. Emotion surges. The mind is pulled away from reflection and back into motion.

Motion restores familiarity. The behavior occurs, often automatically. Afterward, regret arrives—clear, sharp, undeniable. Why did I do that? That's not me. But regret comes after the behavior, not before it. And regret does not restore authority. It reinforces the cycle.

Regret convinces the person that the problem is moral weakness rather than structural interruption. They promise themselves they'll do better next time, resolve to be more careful and more aware. But awareness was never the issue. The issue was that awareness was not allowed to continue.

This is how the cycle tightens. A rational thought appears. Processing is interrupted. Automatic behavior resumes. Regret follows. Self-blame replaces clarity. The system resets. Each cycle deepens the sense of helplessness. People begin to distrust their own thoughts.

They stop believing clarity matters because it never leads anywhere. They learn unconsciously that thinking differently does not change outcomes. So they stop staying with the thought when it arises. They let it pass, distract themselves sooner, and abandon reflection more quickly. This is not laziness. It is conditioning.

The system trains the mind to avoid sustained rational engagement because sustained engagement threatens the pattern, and the pattern must be preserved. This is why people often say they don't know why they keep doing this and that it's like something takes over. They are not being metaphorical.

They are describing loss of continuity between thought and action. The self can recognize but cannot remain, and remaining is what produces change. Without continuity, the mind becomes fragmented. Insight appears in flashes. Action occurs in habits. Regret fills the gap between them.

Because the gap is never closed, the person remains trapped in repetition. They know the behavior is wrong for them. They feel the regret every time. They sense the misalignment clearly. But the system does not allow the insight to progress beyond awareness. It arrests the thought before it becomes disruptive.

This is why telling people to "just think it through" fails. They already are. But thinking is not the same as processing. Processing requires authority. And authority is precisely what has been displaced.

So the person remains in a vicious cycle—aware enough to suffer but not authorized enough to change. This is not a contradiction. It is captivity. Until the interruption itself is addressed, until authority is restored, the cycle will repeat regardless of intelligence, sincerity, or desire.

With each cycle, the space between knowing and doing grows wider, not because the truth weakens but because access to it narrows. The self does not forget. It is simply no longer allowed to intervene. And the system continues—intact, uninterrupted, unquestioned.

At first, regret functions as a signal. It hurts, it stings, and it points backward, saying this wasn't right. People assume regret will eventually prevent repetition, that enough discomfort will produce change. But in captivity, regret is rerouted.

Instead of warning the self before action, it becomes proof after the fact—proof that the person still knows better, still cares, and that something inside them is intact. Because regret feels like awareness, it creates the illusion of agency.

People tell themselves that at least they feel bad and at least they know this isn't them. But regret that arrives only after behavior does not protect the will. It anesthetizes it.

Regret becomes a pressure release, a way to discharge tension without changing direction. The system allows regret because regret does not disrupt momentum. It arrives late, fades quickly, and resets the cycle.

Over time, regret loses its edge—not because the behavior feels right, but because the pattern has trained the mind to expect regret as part of the sequence. Action. Regret. Resolution. Repeat.

The person begins to rely on regret to reassure themselves that they are still themselves. But regret is not authority. It does not initiate, interrupt, or prevent. It simply confirms what has already happened.

This is one of the most deceptive stabilizers of captivity because the person mistakes remorse for resistance. They believe that as long as regret remains, the self is still in control. But control is demonstrated before action, not after it.

When regret becomes proof instead of warning, the system tightens. The person feels awake enough to suffer but never authorized enough to stop. And suffering becomes the evidence they point to when they wonder why nothing changes.

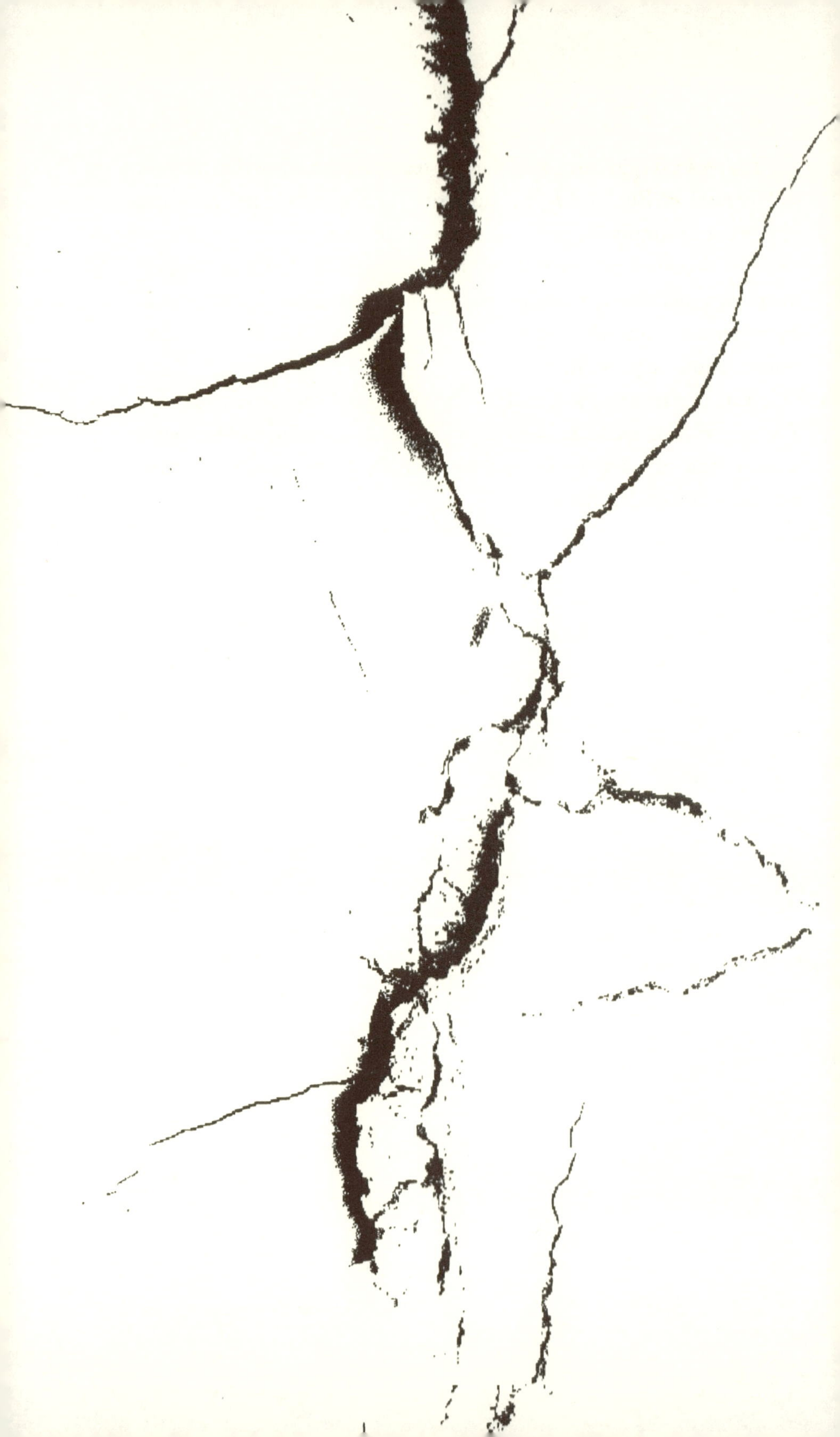

28

THE TURNING POINT

There is a moment many people reach quietly. Not in crisis. Not in despair. But in clarity. It comes after years of trying. They have done the work, explored the explanations, and improved what could be improved. And still, something remains.

At this stage, people are often misdiagnosed as giving up. They are told they are losing hope, that they are burned out, that they need rest. But what is actually happening is different. They are done pretending something works when it doesn't.

The striving ends—not because they don't care, but because effort has reached its limit. This is not collapse. It is accuracy. Exhaustion strips illusion. It removes bravado, performance, and self-deception. The person stops asking what else they can try and begins asking what is actually required.

This question only emerges when the self stops insisting on self-sufficiency. By this point, the pattern is unmistakable. Self-help refined—but did not reclaim. Psychology explained—but did not restore. Medication managed—but did not master. Spirituality comforted—but did not command. None addressed the question of command. None removed the core problem.

This is not an indictment. It is a diagnosis. Many people resist this stage because it feels like defeat. They have been taught that strength means independence, that asking for help is weakness, and that authority must come from within. So they hesitate. They wait. They distract. They try one more method.

But freedom does not arrive through delay. What changes at this moment is not belief. It is posture. The person stops arguing with reality. They acknowledge something simple and unsettling: I cannot remove this myself.

This admission does not weaken the will. It frees it—from pretending to have authority it does not possess. Opposition thrives on self-reliance. As long as the self insists on solving the problem alone, the hierarchy remains inverted. The displaced self continues negotiating with what overrules it.

Exhaustion breaks that cycle. It creates openness—not to new techniques, but to authority. People often expect dramatic desperation before change. But readiness is usually quiet. It sounds like a willingness to be helped, a release of the need to control, and a desire for what actually works.

This is not surrender to despair. It is surrender to truth. Giving up abandons hope. This moment restores it—on different terms. The person stops demanding freedom on their own authority and becomes willing to receive it from a higher one. That shift changes everything.

When striving ends, space opens. Not emptiness—but availability. The defenses that protected pride loosen. The posture that insisted on control softens. The self becomes receptive—not passive. This is not belief yet. It is permission.

Freedom does not begin when you believe harder. It begins when you stop insisting you are the highest authority involved. This is the threshold most people never cross. But those who do find that what resisted them so long does not resist authority it recognizes.

By the time people realize what is happening, leaving no longer feels possible. There is a point where the question is no longer why people don't leave. It is why they can't. By the time occupation is complete, the mechanisms required for escape have already been compromised.

Choice assumes agency. Agency assumes a functioning will. And the will is no longer operating independently. This is the part that is hardest to accept—because it removes comfort. People want to believe that somewhere inside, the self is still fully intact, waiting to rise up at the right moment.

But occupation does not work that way. It does not merely pressure the will. It replaces it. By the time awareness returns, the person is already operating inside a closed system. They may see the truth, feel the ache, and even long for freedom. But longing is not power.

The voice that would normally initiate action has been muted. The internal authority that once said no has been overridden. Even speech can be affected. People know something is wrong, yet cannot articulate it clearly. They sense danger, yet cannot name the source. They feel trapped, yet cannot explain why leaving feels impossible.

This is not confusion. It is restraint. The system does not need to forbid escape. It only needs to neutralize the capacity to initiate it. This is why people remain silent even when silence is destroying them, comply even when compliance feels unbearable, and defend systems they secretly resent.

Not because they agree—but because resistance no longer originates inside them. At this stage, the self is no longer the highest authority within the mind. It still exists. It still observes. It still suffers. But it does not command.

This is captivity, not hesitation. And captivity cannot be undone from within itself. A prison does not generate its own exit. No amount of insight opens a door that does not exist. No amount of awareness restores authority that has been displaced. No amount of effort reclaims a will that is no longer in control.

This is why telling people to "just leave" fails. Why clarity does not produce courage. Why knowing the truth does not automatically make someone free. The self is present—but no longer sovereign.

And until authority is restored from outside the occupied system, escape is not merely unlikely. It is impossible.

29

THE AUTHORITY THAT DEMONS RECOGNIZE

y the time people reach this point, they are no longer interested in theories. They have tried belief systems, practices, and language. What they want now is simple: what actually works.

Many approaches promise power. Rituals, affirmations, declarations, and visualizations can feel intense, focused, even spiritual. But intensity is not authority. These methods depend on the same compromised system they are trying to fix—the self attempting to command from a position it no longer holds.

The result is predictable. The pressure returns. The resistance adapts. The influence remains.

Some people attempt to confront opposition through understanding. They study, analyze, and categorize. But knowledge is descriptive, not directive. Opposition does not leave because it is understood. It leaves when it is commanded by rightful authority.

At this stage, the question becomes unavoidable. What authority does what opposes me actually obey? Not what soothes it. Not what explains it. Not what negotiates with it. What commands it.

True authority does not need to prove itself. It does not argue, escalate, or rely on emotion. It is recognized immediately by what resists the self. This is why certain names provoke reaction—while others are ignored.

Opposition tolerates self-help, psychology, vague spirituality, and moral ambiguity. It adapts to them easily. They do not threaten hierarchy. They leave authority unchallenged.

Across cultures, across histories, across individual experiences, one name produces a different response. Not because of ritual. Not because of volume. Not because of belief strength. But because of authority.

The name is Jesus.

This is not introduced here as theology. It is introduced as fact observed under pressure. Jesus does not negotiate with opposition. He does not integrate it, analyze it, or coexist with it. He commands it. And what resists the human will recognizes that command immediately.

This is critical. People assume the effectiveness of Jesus depends on belief intensity. It does not. Authority is not generated by the believer. It is inherent.

This is why even reluctant, exhausted, skeptical people report the same outcome when they stop asserting themselves and instead appeal to His authority. This conviction points us to the source of power, which does not originate in us. It comes from position.

Modern culture resists the idea of singular authority. It prefers systems, processes, and interpretations. But authority is not democratic. It is hierarchical. And hierarchy is unavoidable in matters of command.

When the self stops trying to manage, explain, or outthink opposition—and instead submits to an authority higher than both—the dynamic changes. Not gradually. Decisively.

What once argued falls silent. What once pressured withdraws. What once resisted no longer has standing. This is not emotional. It is structural.

Submission to rightful authority does not erase the self. It restores it. The will returns. Clarity stabilizes. Resistance becomes possible again. The person does not disappear. They reappear.

This chapter is not an argument for religion. It is an explanation of why authority matters—and why only one authority consistently produces freedom when all others fail. Jesus is not presented here as a belief system. He is presented as the authority that opposition recognizes.

The next chapter addresses the inevitable question: what does freedom actually feel like—once authority is restored? Not perfection. Not constant peace. But something unmistakable—clarity, agency, wholeness, and a sound mind.

30

WHY DELIVERANCE IS QUIET NOW AND WHY THAT'S INTENTIONAL

Many people expect deliverance to be dramatic. They imagine shouting, convulsions, public displays, and a visible clash between forces. When that doesn't happen, they assume nothing has changed. But modern deliverance is often quiet by design—not because the power is weaker, but because the strategy is different.

Deliverance is no longer aimed at spectacle. It is aimed at restoration. In earlier eras, possession was often externalized. Manifestations were obvious. Authority had to be demonstrated publicly because the world itself understood hierarchy. Deliverance functioned as confrontation in plain sight. That context has changed.

Today, the primary battleground is internal. Control is subtle. Compliance is psychological. Authority is eroded quietly rather than challenged openly. So deliverance meets the problem where it exists now—not where people expect it to look like it used to.

Most modern captivity does not scream. It numbs, distracts, fragments, and exhausts. Accordingly, deliverance does not arrive as chaos. It arrives as clarity. This is why many people miss it. They are waiting for intensity. What they receive is coherence. They expect an emotional surge. What returns instead is authorship. They assume freedom will feel explosive. Instead, it feels calm, grounded, and strangely ordinary.

That ordinariness is not weakness. It is authority restored.

Deliverance today often looks like a thought reaching completion, a pause before action, a temptation losing urgency, or a "no" that finally holds. It looks like stillness no longer feeling threatening, like silence no longer producing pressure, like the mind no longer being crowded by voices that argue, rush, or interrupt. Nothing dramatic happened—and yet everything changed.

This quietness is intentional. Dramatic manifestations can actually reinforce captivity in a culture trained to chase stimulation. Noise can be mistaken for power. Emotional intensity can be confused with authority. But authority does not need volume. Authority establishes order.

When Jesus cast out demons during His ministry, the reactions were often visible—not because He required spectacle, but because the opposition was unhidden. The authority was the same then as it is now. What has changed is not the power. It is the hiding place.

Today, influence embeds itself in identity, habit, language, and thought patterns. It hides behind normalcy. It wears the mask of personality, coping, trauma, or temperament. If deliverance arrived loudly in this context, it would bypass the very place restoration must occur: the will.

Deliverance now restores command rather than creating display. It gives the person back their inner position instead of overpowering their body. That is why many people walk away unsure whether anything happened—until they realize days later that something fundamental is different. They are no longer bracing themselves internally. They are no longer negotiating every decision. They are no longer being rushed toward actions they don't endorse. The pressure is gone—not suppressed, but removed.

Quiet deliverance also protects the person. Spectacle externalizes the experience. It can replace one form of loss of control with another. It can make freedom feel dependent on memory, adrenaline, or emotion. Quiet restoration roots freedom internally. The person does not need to relive an event to stay free. They live from restored authority instead.

This is why many people who experience real deliverance struggle to explain it to others. They don't have a story that sounds impressive. They don't have visuals. They don't have a dramatic testimony. They just have their mind back. And that is harder to describe—but far more powerful.

This is also why deliverance often feels anticlimactic at first. People expect a before-and-after contrast that is obvious. Instead, the contrast is subtle but total. Before: pressure governed action. After: choice does. Before: resistance was theoretical. After: resistance functions. Before:

clarity appeared too late. After: clarity arrives in time. This shift does not announce itself. It simply becomes reality.

Quiet deliverance also removes the opportunity for self-deception. If freedom arrived through spectacle, people could attribute it to emotion, suggestion, or temporary intensity. When freedom arrives through restored agency, there is no such confusion. The person knows. They are present again.

This is also why quiet deliverance often precedes confidence. The will returns before fluency. At first, people may feel cautious. They may move slowly. They may test their own responses. This is not weakness. It is recalibration. A system that has been overridden does not immediately trust its own authority. That trust rebuilds through lived experience—each time the person chooses freely, resists successfully, and acts without pressure. Confidence grows naturally. No force is required.

Quiet deliverance also aligns with how God restores rather than replaces. God does not override the human will to free it. He restores it to its rightful position under His authority. That restoration feels peaceful, not violent—ordered, not chaotic.

This is why many people describe deliverance as a sense of "being back" rather than being changed. They don't become someone else. They stop being displaced. The self returns home.

The enemy prefers noise. Noise distracts. Noise destabilizes. Noise keeps attention external. Quiet restoration removes attention from the struggle and returns it to life. This is intentional. Deliverance is not meant to become the center of a person's identity. Freedom is.

The goal is not to be someone who was delivered. The goal is to be someone who lives. That is why deliverance today often feels almost hidden. It slips past expectations, bypasses performance, and avoids spectacle. And in doing so, it restores what was actually taken: authority, continuity, presence, and a sound mind.

Quiet deliverance is not a downgrade. It is precision. It removes what does not belong without disturbing what does. And once it is complete, there is nothing left to watch—only something left to live.

31

157

JESUS AND THE RESTORATION OF THE SELF

When authority is restored, the change is not theatrical. There is no constant emotional surge, no permanent high, and no altered personality. What returns first is something quieter—and unmistakable. The self comes back online.

People often expect freedom to feel dramatic. Instead, it feels clear. Thoughts slow down—not because they are suppressed, but because they are no longer crowded. Inner noise recedes. Mental pressure lifts. The urgency that once drove behavior loses its grip. For the first time in a long while, the person can pause—and remain present.

This is not emptiness. It is command.

One of the clearest signs of restoration is the return of resistance. Not resistance to life—but resistance to what does not belong. A thought arises and can be dismissed. An impulse surfaces and can be refused. A temptation appears and can be evaluated. The internal "no" is no longer theoretical. It functions.

This is not perfection. It is agency.

Before, resistance felt exhausting. Now, it feels proportional. The person no longer has to overpower internal pressure. They simply recognize it—and it loses leverage. This is because authority has shifted. The self is no longer negotiating with opposition. It is aligned under a higher command.

As this alignment settles, fragmentation begins to heal naturally. Thought reconnects to conscience. Emotion reconnects to meaning. Will reconnects to action. The person feels whole—not idealized, not flawless, but internally coherent. There is continuity again.

Shame begins to lose its grip. Shame thrives where authority is absent. Once authority is restored, shame loses its function. Mistakes still register. Conviction still exists. Responsibility remains. But condemnation no longer governs. The person can acknowledge error without collapse. Correction replaces accusation.

This freedom does not come from the self becoming stronger than everything else. It comes from the self being rightly ordered.

Jesus does not overpower the person's will. He restores it. The person does not feel dominated. They feel grounded.

Behavior often changes—but as a result, not a goal. Compulsions weaken. Habits lose urgency. Patterns break. Not because the person is trying harder—but because the internal pressure driving them has been removed. Effort is no longer spent resisting chaos. It is spent living.

One of the most surprising changes many people notice is their relationship with stillness. Silence no longer feels threatening. Quiet no longer provokes agitation. Solitude becomes restorative again. Stillness no longer exposes chaos. It reveals order.

This does not mean the struggle disappears forever. Stress still occurs. Temptation still arises. Choices still matter. But the struggle has changed shape. The person is no longer fighting from inside captivity. They are fighting from freedom.

This restoration does not come from invoking a name as a technique. It comes from relationship. Jesus is not a tool to be used. He is an authority to be aligned with. This alignment is not abstract. It is lived—daily, practically, and quietly.

Perhaps the most profound change is this: the person feels like themselves again. Not a perfected version. Not a fabricated identity. The same self—returned.

Memories make sense again. Values regain weight. Choices feel meaningful. The inner world feels inhabited—by the right authority.

Jesus does not erase who you are. He restores who you are meant to be—by removing what never belonged.

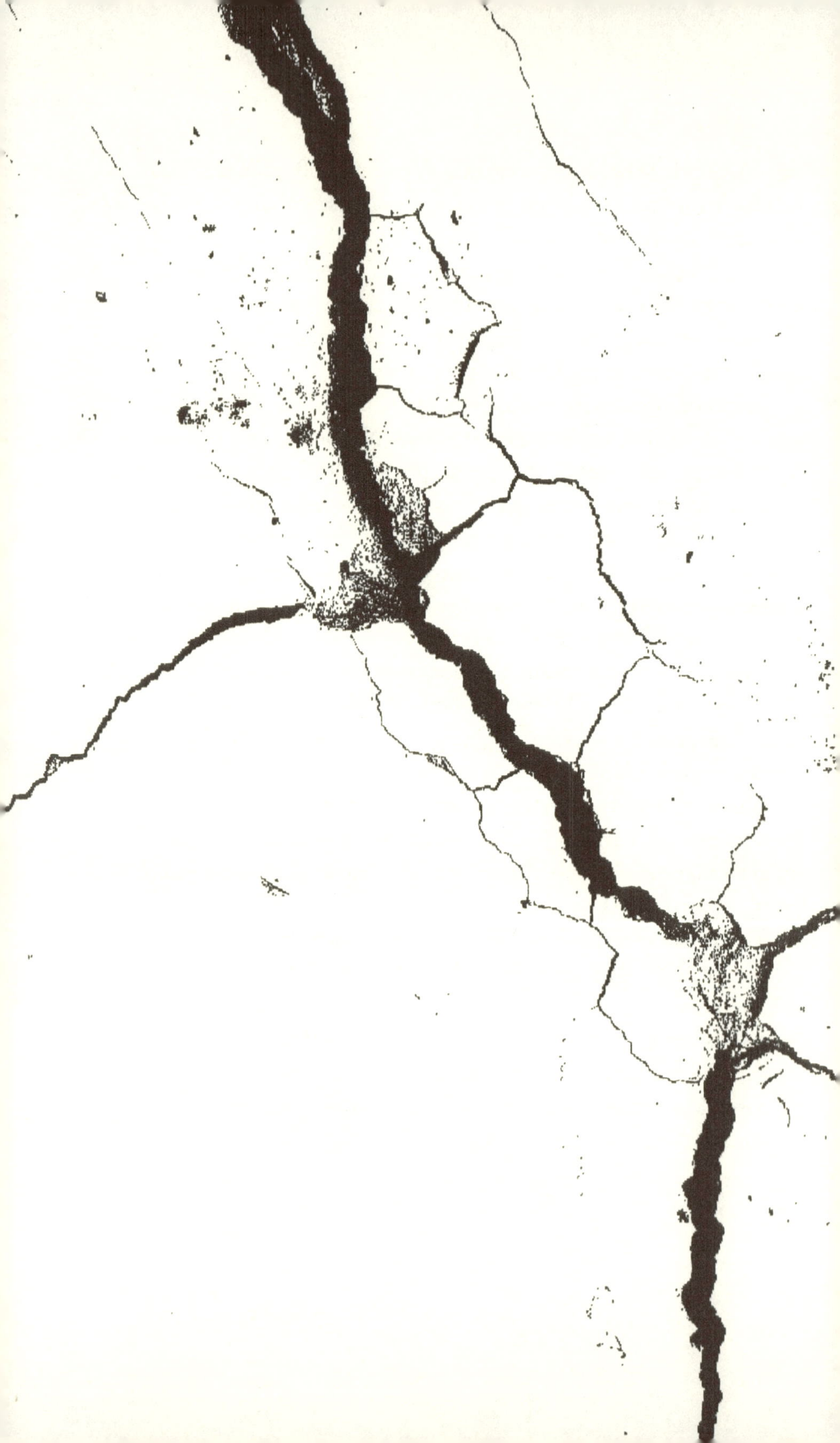

32

WHAT FREEDOM ACTUALLY FEELS LIKE

Freedom is often imagined as intensity—euphoria, overwhelming relief, a sudden and permanent sense of peace. That is not what most people experience. What they experience is something quieter—and far more durable.

Freedom feels like clarity that does not require effort. Thoughts still come. Emotions still arise. But they no longer pile up or compete for dominance. The mind feels ordered, not empty. There is space between impulse and action again—not forced space, but natural space. The person no longer feels constantly pulled. They feel present.

One of the most noticeable changes is what is no longer there. The urgency fades. The pressure lifts. The sense of being driven disappears. Life still has demands—but those demands no longer arrive with internal compulsion. Decisions feel like decisions again.

Before, everything felt exaggerated. Small triggers caused outsized reactions. Minor choices felt overwhelming. Delay felt intolerable. As freedom settles in, proportion returns. What matters feels important. What does not matter loses urgency. This is not emotional flattening. It is accuracy.

The ability to say no returns—and it works. Not harshly. Not reactively. Simply firmly. A thought can be dismissed without argument. A temptation can be declined without drama. A distraction can be ignored without resentment. The self no longer needs to defend every boundary. Authority does that.

The peace that accompanies freedom is not fragile. It may be disturbed—but it is not destroyed. Because it does not depend on circumstances. It depends on alignment. When alignment is intact, pressure does not escalate into panic. Discomfort does not spiral into chaos. Difficulty remains difficulty—but it no longer disorients the self.

Discernment sharpens—not suspicion, not paranoia, but discernment. The person becomes more aware of what belongs and what does not, internally and externally. Influences are noticed earlier. Boundaries are recognized faster. Resistance feels appropriate rather than exhausting. This awareness is calm.

Emotional range returns. Numbness recedes. Joy feels clean. Sadness feels honest. Anger feels purposeful rather than volatile. Emotion reconnects to meaning. The person is not ruled by feeling—but they are no longer disconnected from it either.

One of the most relieving changes is the end of constant internal argument. The endless debating, the justifying, the bargaining—it stops. Not because the person won the argument, but because the argument no longer has authority. The mind grows quieter—not because it is suppressed, but because it is settled.

Freedom does not mean perfection. Temptation still appears. Mistakes still happen. Life still requires effort. But authorship is restored. The person knows, "I am choosing this," or, "I am choosing against this." That knowledge alone changes everything.

Freedom produces a specific kind of confidence. Not arrogance. Not certainty about everything. But steadiness. The person no longer feels easily swayed, hijacked, or internally divided. They feel anchored. This anchoring allows engagement with life without fear of being overtaken by it.

Many people are surprised by how ordinary freedom feels. There is no constant awareness of victory. No dramatic sense of triumph. Life simply feels livable again. That ordinariness is the proof.

Occupation thrives on intensity. Freedom restores normalcy.

This chapter has described what freedom feels like from the inside. What remains is not how to chase it—but how to live from it. Not through obsession. Not through constant vigilance. But through grounded, alert living.

Because freedom is not fragile when it is rightly ordered.

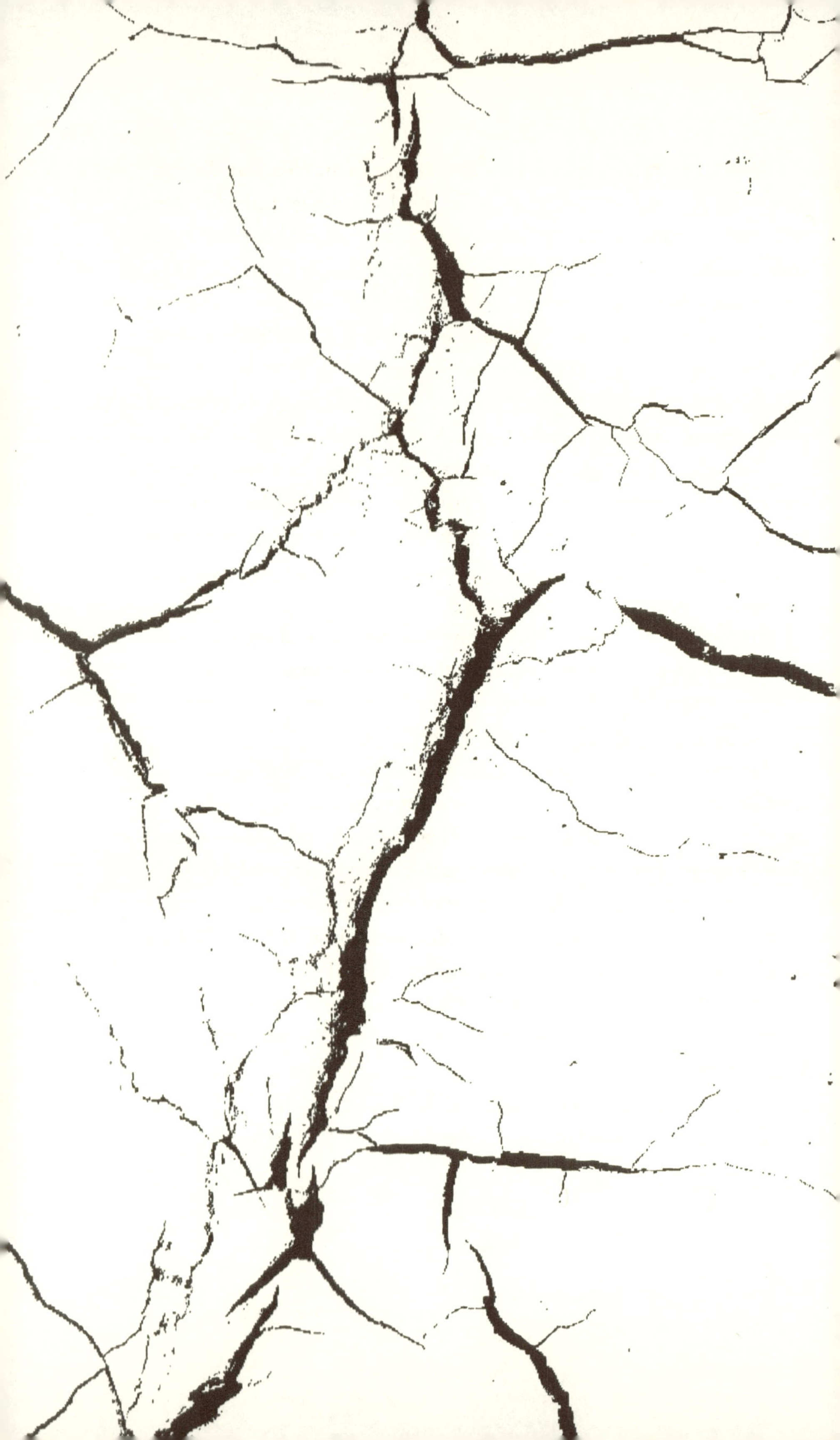

33

STAYING FREE

reedom does not require constant defense. It does not demand hypervigilance, suspicion, or fear, nor is it maintained through obsession or endless self-monitoring. Freedom is sustained through order. When authority is rightly aligned, freedom becomes the default state—not a fragile achievement that must be protected at all costs.

Many people assume that once freedom is restored, they must remain on guard at all times. They watch their thoughts relentlessly, analyze every feeling, and fear slipping back. This posture misunderstands how freedom works. The problem is not self-monitoring—Scripture commands vigilance. The problem is fear replacing authority. Fear fragments and anxiety destabilizes. Watchfulness under God strengthens freedom, while watchfulness without Him recreates strain. Freedom is not maintained by fear; it is maintained by grounded alignment.

Staying free is not complicated. It does not require new techniques or constant effort. It requires staying aligned with the same authority that restored freedom in the first place—not perfectly, not dramatically, but consistently. Alignment is relational rather than mechanical. It is lived out quietly through attention, honesty, and obedience in ordinary moments.

Awareness still matters, but it changes shape. Instead of scanning for threats, the person begins to notice drift. Subtle signs appear: increasing agitation, avoidance of stillness, resentment toward truth, and erosion of restraint. These are not reasons for panic; they are signals to reorient. Correction happens early, before pressure builds.

Stillness, once avoided, becomes protective. Time without distraction allows alignment to be checked naturally. Silence reveals whether authority is still centered or whether something else has begun to crowd in. Stillness does not invite intrusion; it exposes it. This is why a grounded life includes space—unrushed, undistracted, honest space.

Freedom is not maintained through dramatic declarations. It is maintained through small, consistent obedience: choosing truth over convenience, resisting small compromises, and honoring conscience before pressure escalates. These choices are not burdensome; they are stabilizing. They keep hierarchy intact.

Resistance may still appear. This does not mean freedom is gone; it means life is happening. The difference now is response. The person no longer argues endlessly, negotiates, or panics. They return to alignment. Authority handles what the self no longer needs to manage.

Freedom also does not thrive in isolation. It thrives in honesty—not performance, not image, but honesty. Isolation allows drift to go unnoticed, while honest connection restores perspective. This does not require constant disclosure, only a refusal to live divided.

Peace should not be confused with complacency. Complacency ignores alignment; peace rests in it. Staying free means remaining attentive rather than anxious, rooted rather than reactive. Over time, freedom stops feeling like a condition you manage and becomes the ground you stand on.

Life still challenges. Pressure still comes. Choices still matter. But the self remains present, coherent, and governed. This is what stability looks like.

This book has never been about fear; it has been about clarity. Clarity restores agency, agency restores responsibility, and responsibility restores dignity. Nothing in this book requires performance. There is no pressure, no manipulation, no urgency—only honesty.

If you recognized yourself in these pages, then you already know what does not work and what does. The door is not forced; it is simply open. Freedom is not something you maintain by effort. It is something you live from, once the right authority is in place. Freedom is not escape from life; it is the ability to live it whole.

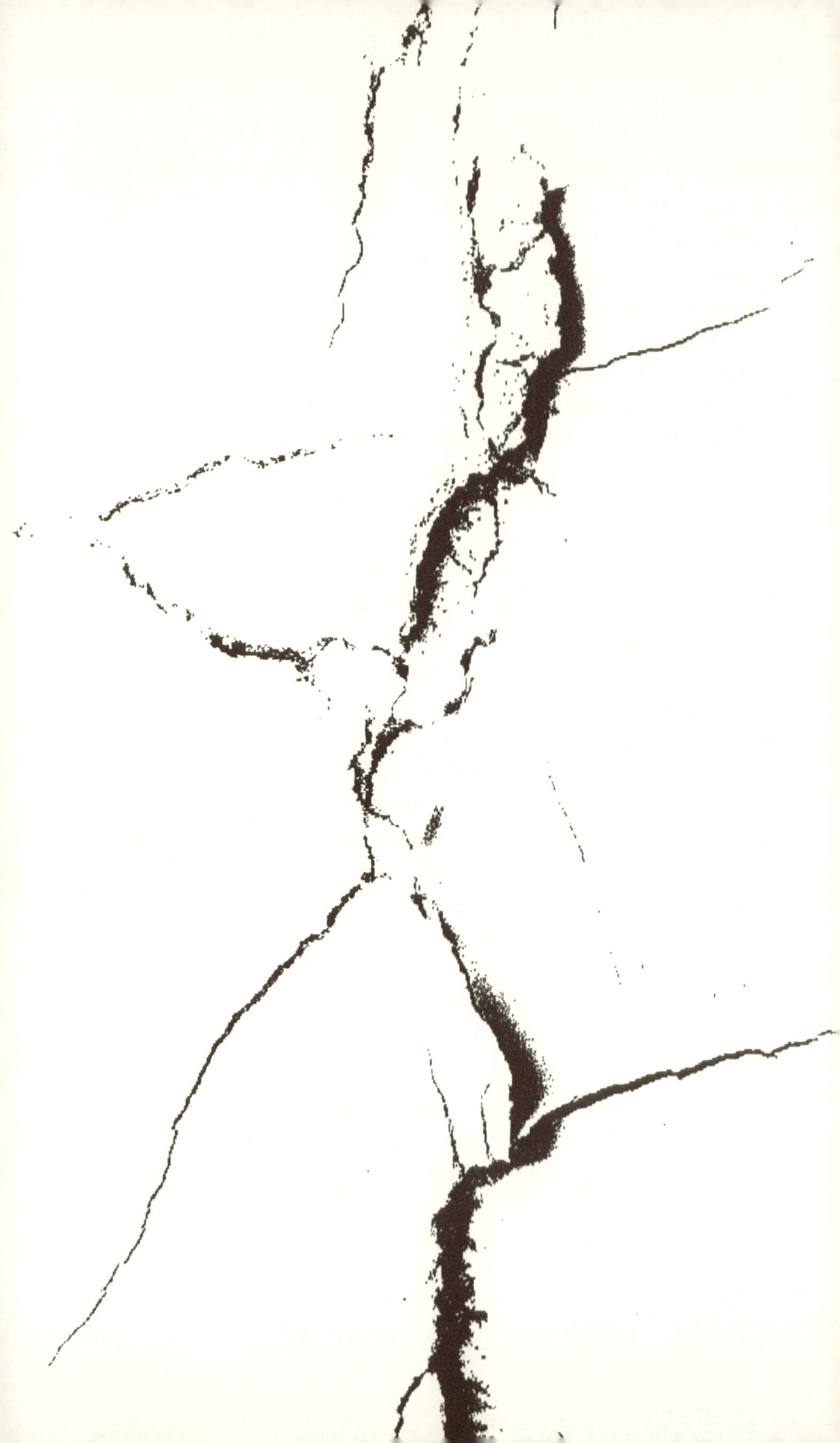

EPILOGUE

WHY RESCUE MUST COME FROM OUTSIDE THE SYSTEM

Once captivity is understood, a dangerous misunderstanding must be avoided. This is not a book about effort. It is not a call to self-improvement, nor is it an argument for stronger willpower or clearer thinking. Those tools assume the will is still sovereign. But occupation does not leave sovereignty intact.

By the time the self recognizes what has happened, it is already operating under authority that does not originate from within. The system is closed. The exit is not accessible from the inside. This is why encouragement fails, why advice feels hollow, and why motivation exhausts rather than empowers. They all speak to a part of the person that no longer holds command.

Rescue, by definition, cannot originate from the place of captivity. A trapped mind cannot liberate itself any more than a locked room can generate its own key. This is not condemnation; it is clarity. The inability to break free is not a personal failure—it is a condition. And conditions require intervention, not guidance, not insight, not affirmation, but intervention.

Something—or someone—must enter the system with authority the system does not possess: authority that is not subject to its rules, authority that is not impaired by its constraints, authority that can speak where speech has been restricted and command where the will has been displaced. Only then does liberation become possible.

This is where the modern conversation usually ends, because it has no language for rescue. But rescue is exactly what is required, and rescue has a name. If the problem were ignorance, education would be enough. If the problem were fear, courage would solve it. If the problem were weakness, discipline would restore strength. But the problem is captivity, and captivity does not respond to advice.

Jesus does not enter this story as a philosophy, a lifestyle, or a belief system. He enters as a rescuer—not working with the occupied will, but replacing the authority that displaced it. This is why self-liberation fails and always will. Freedom does not come from strengthening the self; it comes from surrendering authority to someone who was never subject to the occupation in the first place.

If you recognize yourself in these pages—if you see the captivity, feel the silence, and know you cannot escape it on your own—then the path forward is not effort. It is rescue. Jesus is not one solution among many. He is the only one not operating from inside the occupied system, and that is why He alone can set you free.

And quietly, but unmistakably, something else has been shown as well: authority matters. Not authority as domination, but authority as rightful rule. Jesus is not presented here as a concept, a philosophy, or a religious system. He is the Creator God—the One who made you, who understands the human will because He designed it, and whose authority is higher than anything that opposes it. He does not negotiate with what destroys you. He does not coexist with it. He commands it. And what resists you recognizes His authority.

This invitation is often misunderstood. Freedom begins with alignment, and that alignment is not abstract—it is personal. It means acknowledging that Jesus is Lord, not as a symbolic idea, but as rightful authority over your life. It means repenting of sin, not as self-condemnation, but as clarity—turning away from what has distorted, divided, and displaced you, and agreeing with truth about what does not belong. Repentance is not humiliation; it is reordering.

If you are ready, it begins simply: by asking Jesus to be the Lord of your life, by turning away from sin and agreeing with His authority, by surrendering the struggle to the One who can actually command what opposes you. Not because you are weak, but because you are done pretending you are the highest authority involved.

This is not joining a religion, not performing goodness, not earning freedom. It is returning to rightful order. Jesus does not erase who you are. He restores who you are—by removing what never belonged.

Readiness does not feel dramatic. It sounds like, "I'm done managing this." "I want truth, not substitutes." "I want my life back—under the authority that made me." If that is where you are, you already know what to do—not because it was forced, but because it became clear.

Nothing you experienced was random. Nothing that opposed your wholeness had rightful authority over you. Freedom was never about becoming someone else. It was about returning to who you are—under the Lordship of the One who made you.

A NECESSARY FINAL NOTE

I f you have read this book and recognized patterns of occupation, passivity, loss of resistance, or inward compromise, I want to speak plainly. If you believe this book cannot apply to you because you consider yourself "saved," I urge you to pause.

Scripture does not tell us to assume salvation. It tells us to examine it. "Work out your own salvation with fear and trembling." — Philippians 2:12

Salvation is not proven by a label, a prayer from the past, church attendance, or correct beliefs. It is proven by submission to Jesus Christ as Lord.

Jesus is not presented in this book as an accessory to healing or a comforting idea layered onto self-effort. He is presented as who He is: the Creator God, rightful Lord, and the only authority I have ever seen consistently restore the human will when everything else fails. This is not a theoretical claim. It is an observed one.

If you are reading this and recognizing patterns of occupation, passivity, loss of resistance, or inward compromise—and yet you feel confident saying this can't be me—that confidence itself should be examined.

If Jesus is not Lord of your life—if you have not repented, surrendered, and been made new—then you are not saved.

Do not reason your way around this moment. Do not delay.

Ask Jesus to save you now. Call on Him. Repent of your sins. Submit your life to Him fully. He is not distant. He is not withholding. But He will not be assumed.

This book is not written to condemn you. It is written to wake you up. And if this warning unsettles you, that is not fear to suppress. That is fear to listen to.

APPENDIX

SCRIPTURE REFERENCES

All Scripture quotations are from the King James Version (KJV) of the Bible.

ON SPIRITUAL AUTHORITY, THOUGHT, AND SALVATION

Ephesians 6:12

> For we wrestle not against flesh and blood, but against principalities, against powers, against the rulers of the darkness of this world, against spiritual wickedness in high places.

John 3:16

> For God so loved the world, that he gave his only begotten Son, that whosoever believeth in him should not perish, but have everlasting life.

Philippians 4:8

> Finally, brethren, whatsoever things are true, whatsoever things are honest, whatsoever things are just, whatsoever things are pure, whatsoever things are lovely, whatsoever things are of good report; if there be any virtue, and if there be any praise, think on these things.

2 Corinthians 10:5–6

> Casting down imaginations, and every high thing that exalteth itself against the knowledge of God, and bringing into captivity every thought to the obedience of Christ;
> And having in a readiness to revenge all disobedience, when your obedience is fulfilled.

Philippians 2:12

> Wherefore, my beloved, as ye have always obeyed, not as in my presence only, but now much more in my absence, work out your own salvation with fear and trembling.

ON POSSESSION, UNCLEAN SPIRITS, AND DELIVERANCE

Mark 5:8

> For he said unto him, Come out of the man, thou unclean spirit.

Mark 5:15

> And they come to Jesus, and see him that was possessed with the devil, and had the legion, sitting, and clothed, and in his right mind: and they were afraid.

Luke 8:30

> And Jesus asked him, saying, What is thy name? And he said, Legion: because many devils were entered into him.

Luke 9:42

> And as he was yet a coming, the devil threw him down, and tare him. And Jesus rebuked the unclean spirit, and healed the child, and delivered him again to his father.

Matthew 12:43–45

> When the unclean spirit is gone out of a man, he walketh through dry places, seeking rest, and findeth none.
> Then he saith, I will return into my house from whence I came out; and when he is come, he findeth it empty, swept, and garnished. Then goeth he, and taketh with himself seven other spirits more wicked than himself, and they enter in and dwell there: and the last state of that man is worse than the first. Even so shall it be also unto this wicked generation.

Acts 10:38

> How God anointed Jesus of Nazareth with the Holy Ghost and with power: who went about doing good, and healing all that were oppressed of the devil; for God was with him.

2 Timothy 2:26

> And that they may recover themselves out of the snare of the devil, who are taken captive by him at his will.

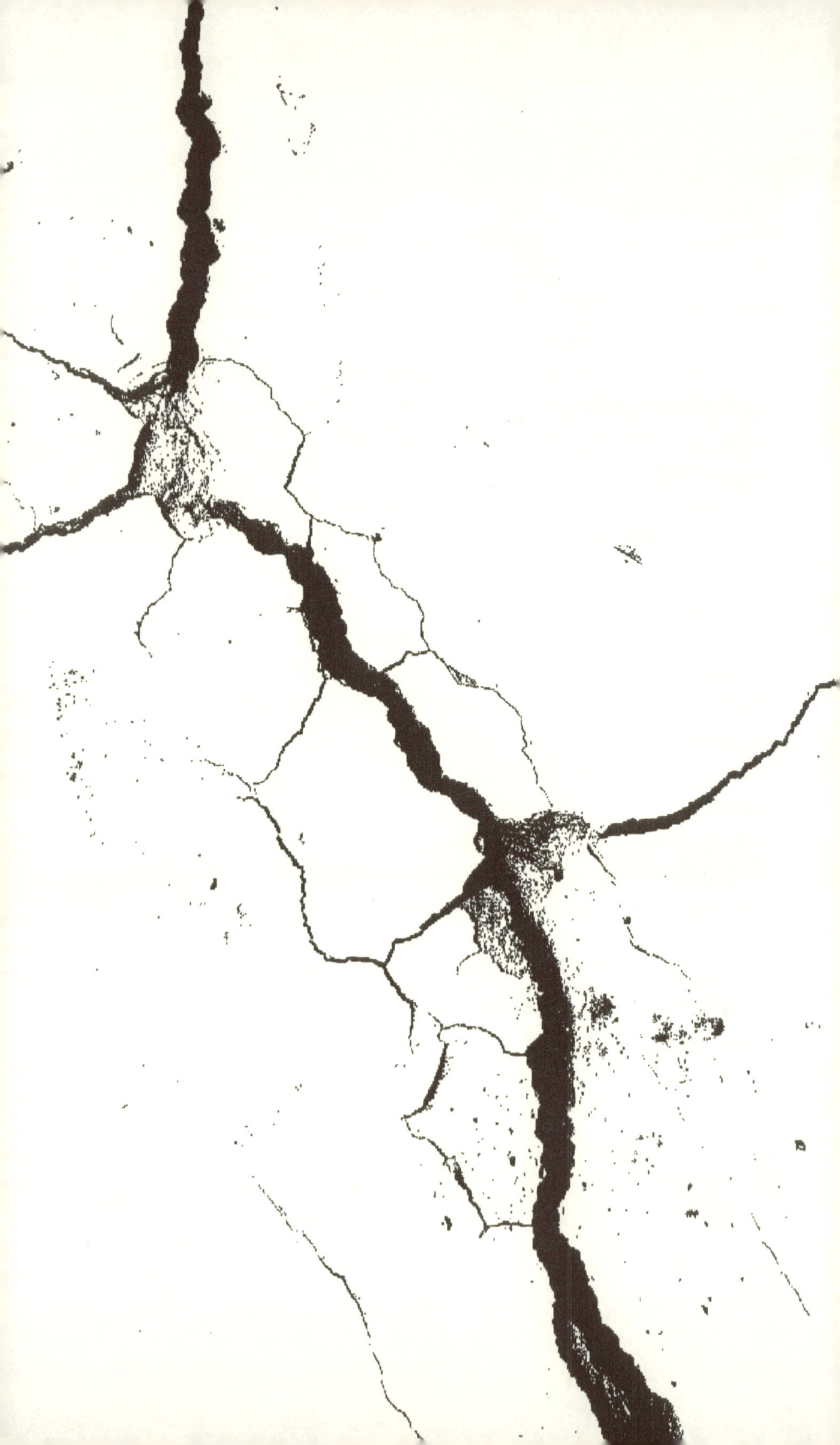

ABOUT THE AUTHOR

Jackleine Spring is an author whose work focuses on clarity, discernment, and the restoration of human agency in an increasingly disordered world. Her writing examines the subtle ways authority is displaced, truth is obscured, and identity is gradually overtaken without resistance.

She is also the author of Real Life Anti-Aging Health Strategies, which explores physical vitality, mental clarity, and long-term wellness through grounded, real-world practices.

Jackleine Spring writes and publishes through Solid Ground House Publishing™.

SOLIDGROUNDHOUSEPUBLISHING.COM
